John Deere Buggies and Wagons

Ralph C. Hughes

Published by the
American Society of Agricultural Engineers
St. Joseph, Michigan

About ASAE — The Society for engineering in agricultural, food, and biological systems

ASAE is a technical and professional organization of members committed to improving agriculture through engineering. Many of our 8,000 members in the United States, Canada, and more than 100 other countries are engineering professionals actively involved in designing the farm equipment that continues to help the world's farmers feed the growing population. We're proud of the triumphs of the agriculture and equipment industry. ASAE is dedicated to preserving the record of this progress for others. This book joins many other popular ASAE titles in recording the exciting developments in agricultural equipment history.

John Deere Buggies and Wagons
Editor and Book Designer: Melissa Carpenter Miller
Cover Designer: Bill Thompson

Library of Congress Catalog Number (LCCN) 95-83107
International Standard Book Number (ISBN) 0-929355-71-7

Printed in the U.S.A.

Acknowledgments

The resources of the Deere & Company Archives and the dedicated assistance of reference librarian Vicki Eller and archivist Les Stegh made this book possible. With computers, they searched the Deere historic records for a variety of reference material; first on buggies, then on wagons. One reference led to another: first to literature 75 years old, then to sales catalogs printed more than 100 years ago. There were old copies of *The Furrow* and *The Farm Implement News* to thumb through, and stacks of Deere & Company Annual Reports to peruse, even minutes of Deere board of directors meetings to scan.

Searching for suitable illustrations was a rewarding challenge, especially since much of the reference material was printed in the early days of photography. Many of the pictures selected are hand-sketched, color illustrations. Copying these old illustrations so they could be clearly reproduced on a modern offset printing press was a task capably handled by the Deere & Company Photo Department. Many "thanks" to them!

Credit also should be extended to Donna Hull and Melissa Miller of the ASAE for considering the author's manuscript worthy of publishing; and for producing a book that is not only inviting to look at, but also easy to read.

Ralph C. Hughes, author

About the Author

Ralph Hughes was born in Indiana where he spent much time on his family's farm. He graduated from the School of Agriculture at Purdue University. He remained at Purdue to work for both the Agricultural Extension Service and the Agricultural Experiment Station, editing information bulletins and writing news releases. He joined Deere & Company in 1954, starting as a writer for *The Furrow*, the Company's farm magazine. Later, he wrote advertising copy for a variety of John Deere products, including farm and industrial tractors, lawn and garden tractors, corn planters, grain drills, manure spreaders, and farm wagons.

In 1984, he was appointed Director of Advertising, the position from which he retired in 1992. During his 38 years of service, he not only learned much about John Deere products, but also about Deere & Company's history. Several of his articles have appeared in *Green Magazine* and he has contributed material to the *Two Cylinder magazine*. Ralph Hughes also has written two other books about John Deere: The first was on two-cylinder tractors and entitled, *How Johnny Popper Replaced the Horse*; and the second was about John Deere scale-model toy tractors, *The Toy and the Real McCoy*.

Preface

The year is 1880. The United States and Canada are predominately rural societies. Immigrants by the thousands are boarding trains in the East for points West: Cincinnati, Chicago, Minneapolis, St. Louis, Kansas City, and Toronto — even Moline, Illinois. Every town wants to be "on the railroad." Sternwheelers are on all the navigable rivers. "Automobile," "tractor," and "airplane" are words that don't yet exist.

It's still a man's world! Civil War veterans — blue and gray — are holding reunions and shaking hands at Gettysburg. Words like "congressman," "policeman," "fireman," "postman," and "third-baseman" are still politically correct. There are even words without "man" in them that are strictly masculine: "conductor," "officer," "miner," "bartender," "pitcher and catcher." John Deere still strolls through his plow factory, but his son, Charles, is now the boss. He, Stephen Velie, and other boardmembers are making plans to expand the Company's marketing ability. They are signing partnership agreements to establish new sales branches. Dealers are being recruited (they were called "agents" back then). Farmers have started to ride on their plows and cultivators; and the Company is developing and seeking other new products.

There's a barn or stable behind most houses. A horse has to be hitched to go to town or for a ride in the country. The bicycle craze is just beginning. The buggy business and wagon trade look promising. Grade school boys can point out the skein, felloes, and hounds on a wood wagon. They also know what a bow or a boot is on a buggy.

The year is now 1920. Farmers know that a Fort Smith Wagon and a Reliance Buggy are quality-built John Deere products. The Planter Works, the Wagon Works, and the Spreader Works have joined the Plow Works as John Deere factories dedicated primarily to one product line. (Today, they are all gone.) In another decade, the John Deere All-Steel Wagon will have rubber tires; replaceable, steel sleeve bearings with zerk grease fittings; a telescoping reach, "auto steering," and a tongue with a tractor hitch.

John Deere was in the buggy business for only 25 years and built wood wagons for just 50 years; yet both product lines are bits of Company history that deserve to preserved. It's a short history; so this is not a thick book. The author doesn't claim to be a buggy or wagon expert. He claims only that the facts gathered from 100-year-old sales catalogs, dusty farm magazines and yellowed Company correspondence are accurately reported for your enlightenment and enjoyment.

Ralph C. Hughes, author

Table of Contents

Part I: Buggies

Part II: Wagons

Part III: Color Pictorial Section: Buggies and Wagons

Part II: Wagons (con't)

Part IV: Appendices

DEERE VEHICLE — DAY OR NIGHT

Part I: Buggies

Few photographs were taken of John Deere buggies or spring vehicles. It's interesting that this photograph, used in a 1909 issue of The Furrow, *also featured an automobile. Note the high arch of the buggy axles, the leather top, rear curtain, and the auto seat.*

Just as many Americans today look to Detroit for automobiles, Americans 100 years ago looked to St. Louis for stylish, high-quality buggies. So, too, did Deere & Company in the early 1900s. And by 1912, buggies were an important segment of Deere's business; farm wagons, too. After World War I, the automobile became more affordable and the buggy business started down the road to oblivion. Wood wagon production was not adversely affected until after World War II. And all-steel farm wagons showed considerable promise, especially after John Deere began selling farm tractors in 1918.

Deere didn't jump into the buggy business; far from it. It's more accurate to say that John Deere backed into the vehicle business through companies it owned, were in partnership with, or had a financial interest in. Shortly after the Civil War, Deere established sales branches in several North American cities through a series of partnerships. The first branch was Deere Mansur & Company of Kansas City. It was followed by Mansur & Tebbetts Implement Company of St. Louis; Deere & Webber of Minneapolis; Deere, Wells & Company in Council Bluffs/Omaha; and the Marcus C. Hawley & Company in San Francisco. All five branches started to sell buggies and wagons before Deere & Company. These sales branches influenced the Company's entrance in both the buggy and wagon trade.

Each sales branch contracted with a number of independent "agents" in mostly small rural communities. (Agents were later called "dealers.") The branches and agents represented the John Deere product line in their respective trade areas. The line at the time consisted mostly of plows, cultivators, harrows, and planters. These branches and agents also represented other manufacturers' products, some of which were directly competitive with Deere.

As early as 1883, Mansur & Tebbetts, the Deere branch in St. Louis, bought "white" (unfinished) buggies, painted and finished them as their agents requested. By 1891, buggy sales reached a level sufficient to justify Mansur & Tebbetts to establish a buggy factory of its own: the Mansur & Tebbetts Carriage Company. As sales continued to grow, it was necessary to move the manufacturing of buggies from one building to another in St. Louis to increase production capacity. By 1903, Mansur &

This illustration is from a 1893 sales catalog of the Mansur & Tebbetts Implement Company, the Deere branch in St. Louis. Buggy and carriage sales in 1890 reached a level at Mansur & Tebbetts to justify starting its own vehicle factory: Mansur & Tebbetts Carriage Manufacturing Company. In 1913, the factory was incorporated as the John Deere Reliance Buggy Company.

The "Youngblood" Driving Buggy was one of several popular models in the Mansur & Tebbets Spring Vehicle line in 1895. The name suggests that this model may have been designed for young men engaged in "Gay Nineties" social activities, such as courting.

White Elephant Buggy Factory

During the few years between the time Deere bought the Mansur & Tebbetts Carriage Company and before it was incorporated as the Reliance Buggy Company, the firm officially was known as the "White Elephant Buggy Factory," and its product line as "White Elephant Vehicles." Obviously, back then, the term "white elephant" didn't have the same negative connotation it has today. Before its purchase, Mansur & Tebbetts used a white elephant in its trademark, much the same as John Deere uses a deer today.

When the sales branch in Omaha — Deere, Wells & Company — decided to sell buggies, it elected to represent two vehicle lines: those manufactured by the Velie Carriage Company of Moline, Illinois, and by the Mansur & Tebbetts Carriage Company of St. Louis. The Velie Carriage Company was formed in 1900 by Willard L. Velie, a grandson of John Deere. Velie had worked for Deere from 1890 to 1900, and continued to serve on Deere's board of directors until 1921. The Omaha sales branch represented both vehicle lines even after Deere & Company purchased Mansur & Tebbetts and formed the Reliance Buggy Company. In contemporary terms, the

Tebbetts occupied a plant known locally as the "Sunlight Factory," because it was so well lighted by several tall windows on all four sides. The building had 150,000 square feet and was equipped to manufacture 30,000 vehicles annually.

Deere Acquires A Buggy Factory

On August 17, 1899, Deere & Company dissolved its partnership with the Mansur & Tebbetts Implement Company by purchasing all of the shares owned by other stockholders. Included in the purchase was the Mansur &

Tebbetts Carriage Company. Deere was now in the buggy business. The Mansur & Tebbetts Implement Company name was changed in 1901 to the John Deere Plow Company of St. Louis. In 1913, the vehicle manufacturing business was separated from the Plow Company and incorporated under the name of Reliance Buggy Company. By now, most John Deere branches were selling buggies, carriages, and surreys built by the Reliance Buggy Company. Some branches continued selling other brands of buggies and spring vehicles.

After Deere purchased the Mansur & Tebbetts Carriage Manufacturing Company, and before it was incorporated as the Reliance Buggy Company, the property was called the "White Elephant Buggy Factory." A white elephant had been used in the Mansur & Tebbetts trademark.

Velie was the "Cadillac" and Deere the "Chevrolet" of the buggy trade.

C.C. Webber, manager of Deere & Webber in Minneapolis, was less enthusiastic about the buggy business. In a letter to the new manager of the San Francisco sales branch, he said: "In the hustle for wagon and buggy trade, none of us want to overlook the fact that the plow trade is our principal mission." The Minneapolis sales branch, however, along with Deere Mansur & Company in Kansas City, did represent the Mansur & Tebbetts line; and later, sold vehicles from the Reliance Buggy Company. By 1912, Reliance-built John Deere vehicles were sold in every state in the Union. Less than a decade later, the automobile was starting to write an obituary for buggies and Deere was making plans to exit the buggy business.

Furrow Advertises Buggies

Deere's farm magazine, *The Furrow*, in 1909 published a different edition of each issue for each of the sales branches. This practice gave the branches an opportunity to advertise whatever farm equipment was saleable in their trade area, including different brands of buggies. An ad, for example, in the St. Louis branch edition featured "Deere Vehicles" manufactured at the "John Deere Buggy Factory" in St. Louis. In the Omaha edition of the same *Furrow* issue, there were two full-page ads: one for "Velie Wrought Iron Vehicles" manufactured by the Velie Carriage Company and another ad for "Deere Vehicles" from the "John Deere Sunlight Buggy Factory." The

"Deere Vehicles Stay on the Road"

Style, Finish, Workmanship and Durability Unequaled

DEERE Twin-Auto-Seat

With quick-shift top. Quickly converted into a stylish open driving wagon by removing top.

A Good Buggy is—
A Comfort
A Convenience
A Business Asset

YOU have met a stranger driving a skinny, bony horse hitched to a rickety buggy. You formed a mental picture of his home surroundings. In your mind you can see his tumble-down buildings, weedy fence corners and barren dooryard. It seems clear to you that this man is poor—and still you may be mistaken. Millionaires sometimes live in hovels. But you know how little respect is shown such people.

Another thing, it is hard to correct a bad impression even if wrong.

People are judged by their "turnouts" quite as much as by their clothes.

DEERE VEHICLES

are built for the man who takes pride in what he has and wants to be judged right when away from home.

They are the thoroughbreds of the vehicle world. They have style about them that attracts and satisfies. The springs are "velvety" and the seat comfortable. There is room enough to be cool in summer and for plenty of robes and wraps in winter.

Deere Vehicles have remarkable strength and general staunchness—they will stand rough usage, but pride in their quality will not let you abuse them. You will think more of a **Deere** buggy than of a fine suit of clothes and in the long run you will find a **Deere** much cheaper than an ordinary buggy. Look for the name plate.

Write for our FREE booklet
"The Make-Up of a Good Buggy"
Tells some interesting things about buggy building.

Mention "The Furrow"

WRITE TO

JOHN DEERE PLOW COMPANY
OMAHA, NEB.

The John Deere "Sunlight" Buggy Factory,
Corner Broadway and Clinton Street, St. Louis.
Occupied December 15, 1903. Capacity, 30,000 Vehicles Annually

In 1909, this buggy ad appeared in the Omaha edition of The Furrow, Deere's farm magazine. Style, fine workmanship, and durability were hallmarks of a John Deere Buggy. The St. Louis "Sunlight Factory," pictured here, was one of the largest buggy shops in North America.

This John Deere Reliance buggy ad appeared in a 1920 issue of The Furrow. By the drop in sales, it was obvious that the buggy era was coming to an end and that Deere soon would be exiting the business. An ad for the Model "N" Waterloo Boy Tractor also appeared in this issue.

JOHN DEERE RELIANCE BUGGIES

The life of any vehicle is mainly in the wheels, and the strength of the wheels is in the hubs.

Reliance hubs are special size, designed for strength. They are an improvement on the Sarven patent, being enlarged in the center to give the spokes a longer tenon and greater resistance.

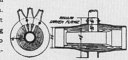

Compare the cross sections of the hubs shown in the illustration. Note the deeper, firmer setting of the spoke tenons. This construction holds the spokes firm when the tires stretch. They do not rattle nor break. And the spokes themselves are heavier.

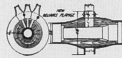

In every feature that stands for real vehicle value, you will find Reliance vehicles uniform in their excellence. Every bit of material that goes into their construction is of the best. It is given the closest inspection before it goes into a buggy. Nothing is retained that does not come up to the high Reliance standard.

See the Reliance buggies at your John Deere dealer's. Write us for booklet fully describing these vehicles. Please mention THE FURROW.

John Deere Plow Company
Moline, Illinois

Minneapolis edition featured both Deere and Velie buggies in the same ad. By 1920, however, the different *Furrow* editions featured only ads for "John Deere Reliance Buggies," along with ads for a wood, two-wheel John Deere Reliance "Auto Trailer." It was available with either a flared box or stock rack.

The John Deere Reliance Buggy Company manufactured a variety of stylish, light-running, one- and two-horse spring vehicles. They were available with seats upholstered in leather, cloth, or whipcord. Tops were available that could be "shifted" (put up or down) quickly. Dashes were padded and there was carpeting on the floor, along with fenders and oil burning lamps for some models. There were several types of vehicles: two-passenger buggies, Phaetons and Concord Wagons; four-passenger surreys, Cabriolets and Spring Wagons; Drummer and delivery wagons. These vehicles were comfortable and "easy riding." They had two to five sets of springs supporting the body, depending on the style, size, and number of passengers carried.

There was also a Rural Mail Wagon in the John Deere line that could be converted for delivering dairy products. It was basically a one-horse spring wagon. The body was 54 inches long and 30 inches wide, "well ironed" and supported by 36-inch elliptic springs in the front and rear. The front wheels were 39 inches high; the rear, 43 inches. It was fully enclosed to protect the driver in all types of weather. It had a full-length, framed top; sliding doors with glass "panels" on both sides; and a hinged glass transom in the front with holes for the reins. In the rear, there was a roll curtain made of coated duck with a small "light" (window) in the center. The dash was fitted with a writing desk and pigeon holes for sorted mail.

The Louisiana Purchase Exposition was held in St. Louis in 1904 to celebrate the 100th anniversary of that important land acquisition, which occurred during the Thomas Jefferson presidency. John Deere displayed several vehicles at the show, but not its complete line.

Even though it looked like a buggy, this spring vehicle was called a "Concord Wagon." Note the long springs located on each side of the body, instead of in the front and rear. Also note the covered boot at the rear of the body; it would be called a "trunk" today.

"Phaeton" was a fancy name for a deluxe, stylish buggy. This model had three springs supporting the body, fenders over the rear wheels, and an oil lamb on each side. The floor was carpeted, dash padded and the foot step had a "non-slip" rubber pad.

Four passengers rode in comfort in this cut-under surrey. Note the short rear fender and "three-quarter" (length) top. A rubber storm apron and side curtains could be stored under the rear seat. A step was provided for the rear-seat passengers; the front-seat passengers had to use the wheel hub as a step.

With platform springs in the rear and the elliptic springs in the front, this Cabriolet (deluxe surrey) was "easy riding." Note how the rear fender extends forward to become the foot step. This family carriage was probably the most expensive vehicle in the John Deere Reliance line in 1900; the price was $300. The oil lamps, storm front, and side curtains were "extras."

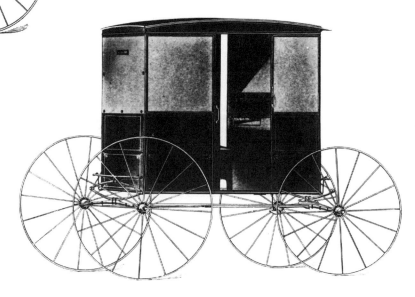

Town wagon, spring wagon, or buckboard — this vehicle was called all three. The body was 6 feet 3 inches long and 31 inches wide (outside) and supported by three elliptic springs. It had a drop endgate and wood dash.

During the first decade of the 20th Century, John Deere included a Rural Mail Wagon in the "White Elephant Vehicle" line. It was equipped with a writing desk and pigeon holes for sorted mail. Dairies also used this fully-enclosed, one-horse spring wagon to deliver milk.

Buggy Construction

The finish of a buggy body was all important. It took two to three months to sand, prime, and paint a vehicle body in preparation for the final coat of varnish. Different sizes of wheels were available with the front wheels being normally 4 inches smaller in diameter than the rear wheels. Common wheel size combinations were 39-43 inches, 36-40 inches, and 42-46 inches. Different wheel widths could be ordered: ¾-, ⅞-, 1-, and 1-⅛-inch were available. The wider wheels were recommended for muddy, country roads; the narrower wheels were considered more stylish and better suited for in-town "driving."

With the paving of rural roads and the bricking of city streets, there came a demand for rubber buggy tires. In its 1920 price list, the John Deere Plow Company of Moline offered two rubber tires as "extra" equipment: a ⅞- or

A buggy looks frail when compared to a wood farm wagon. "Not so" said this photograph that appeared in a 1901 issue of The Farm Implement News. *The nine men sitting on the wheels, body, and top of this John Deere buggy had a combined weight of 1,540 pounds.*

STRONGER THAN THE STRONGEST

WEIGHT OF MEN 1,540 POUNDS

JUST A LITTLE BETTER THAN THE BEST

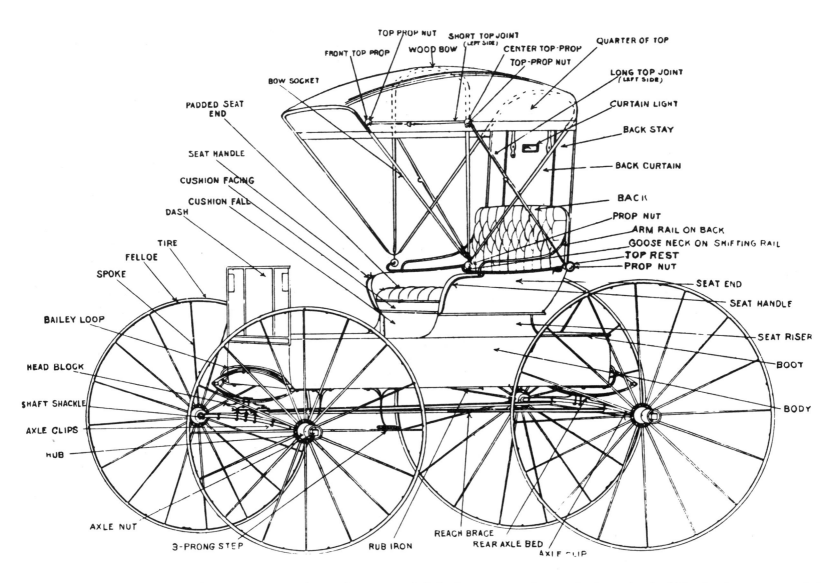

TOP PROP NUT
FRONT TOP PROP
BOW SOCKET
PADDED SEAT END
SEAT HANDLE
CUSHION FACING
CUSHION FALL
DASH
TIRE
FELLOE
SPOKE
BAILEY LOOP
HEAD BLOCK
SHAFT SHACKLE
AXLE CLIPS
HUB
AXLE NUT
3-PRONG STEP
RUB IRON

SHORT TOP JOINT (LEFT SIDE)
WOOD BOW
CENTER TOP-PROP
TOP-PROP NUT
QUARTER OF TOP
LONG TOP JOINT (LEFT SIDE)
CURTAIN LIGHT
BACK STAY
BACK CURTAIN
BACK
PROP NUT
ARM RAIL ON BACK
GOOSE NECK ON SHIFTING RAIL
TOP REST
PROP NUT
SEAT END
SEAT HANDLE
SEAT RISER
BOOT
BODY
REACH BRACE
REAR AXLE BED
AXLE CLIP

Here's an opportunity to become a buggy expert; just learn the names of all the buggy parts. Except for four wheels, fifth-wheel steering, and the use of horses, buggies and wood wagons had little in common. The buggy was built for comfort and speed; the wagon for strength and utility. Buggies, like today's automobiles, were built as stylish and comfortable as possible.

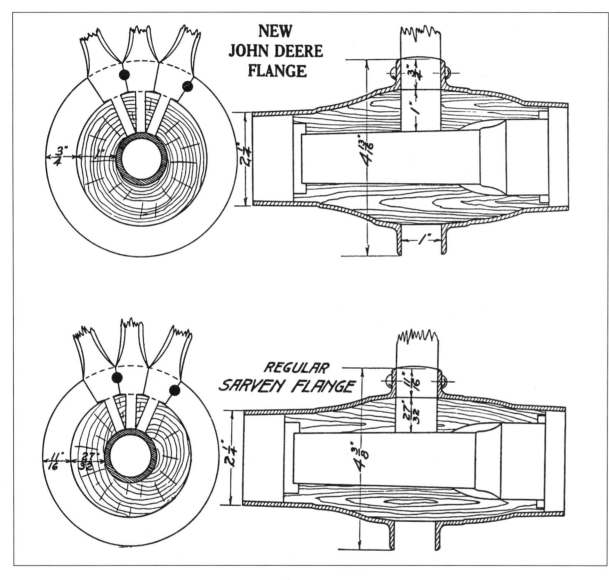

In comparative tests, the John Deere buggy wheel hub proved to be 50 percent stronger than the Sarven hub widely used by competitive buggy companies. The extra strength was due to the longer spoke tenon and the extra thickness of the wood core inside the wheel flange and hub.

1-inch "Goodyear Wing" tire. Steel buggy tires were usually ¼-inch thick. Rubberized horseshoes also became popular to reduce street noise and slippage on hard, paved surfaces.

Wheels, axles, and springs were the "foundation" of a buggy. For a truly stylish appearance, the wheels needed to be slender, but strong; the spokes tapered and securely fastened to the rim or felloes. Every piece of timber used in John Deere wheel construction was air-seasoned and carefully selected. The rims were double screwed at the end of each spoke to prevent splitting. The Reliance Buggy wheel hub was patterned after the well-known Sarven hub design, but was claimed to be 50 percent stronger. The hub center was larger and the spoken tenon and mitre were longer, giving each spoke a deeper and firmer setting in the hub. This design reduced the tendency of the spokes to become loose when the iron tires stretched, which was a common occurrence after a few years of use.

Sturdy Reaches and Axles

Reaches were made of straight-grain hickory, reinforced with high-grade channel iron. Later model John Deere buggies had "twin" (two) reaches securely braced against the rear axle.

In 1912, Reliance buggies were built with a "twin-reach" gear. Each reach was made of hickory and reinforced full length by channel iron. "Stay" braces were "clipped" (attached) to each of the two reaches and to both sides of the rear axle.

malleable iron and the lower supporting parts were made of steel; the rest was wrought iron. The fifth wheel had the king bolt positioned behind the front axle to provide a tight turning radius.

Buggy springs were "full elliptic, 36 inches long, graded and tempered for correct weight capacity and flexibility." In advertising, the claim was that "Deere springs ride easy whether carrying a

Axles were made of high-carbon, heat-treated steel "designed to carry the load with no danger of letting down." Axles were either arched, "dropped," or built in a patented "True-Sweep" pattern. Axles had dustproof, long-wearing spin-dles with 12-inch cone bearings.

The fifth wheel on a Reliance Buggy was 12 inches in diameter to provide a large bearing surface. The top circle was

The "True-Sweep Bike Gear" on John Deere buggies was a patented design feature. It was unique in the way the elliptic spring was combined with the high-arch axle to provide a comfortable ride with less side sway.

The St. Louis edition of the 1909 autumn issue of *The Furrow included this ad for Deere Vehicles. The* "Stay on the Road" *headline referred to the durability and quality of construction; not to the buggy's steering ability.*

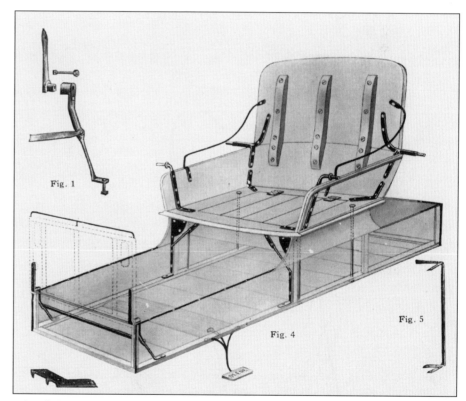

This "ghost" view shows how a John Deere Reliance buggy body, seat, and dash were reinforced with iron parts for added strength and durability.

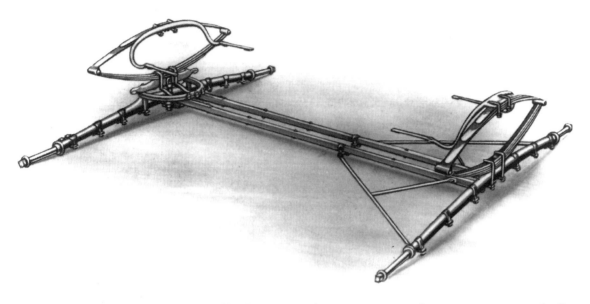

This twin reach gear was used on all John Deere Reliance Buggies and Driving Wagons with elliptic springs. It combined in one gear both strength and flexibility. The design and simplicity of the 12-inch-diameter fifth wheel is shown here.

light or heavy load. It is worth a good deal to have a buggy that won't tire you out on a long journey. And Deere springs will not become lumpy and dead after a little use."

Reliance Buggies and other spring vehicles could be equipped with either shafts (for one horse) or a pole for two horses. Shafts and poles were made of straight-grained hickory. Both were "specially ironed" (reinforced) at points where breakage might occur. Shafts and poles of different designs were offered as optional equipment.

A Quiet Richness

"Style" was an important feature claimed for John Deere vehicles in early advertising and sales literature. Then, as today, "style" was difficult to define and quantify. Deere used such phrases as "pleasing outward appearance;" "a quiet richness that grows on you;" "a rich, durable finish;" "neat, roomy design," and "a handsome piece of work" to describe the style of its spring vehicles. The design of John Deere Reliance Buggies by 1910 started to reflected a few of the design features of the early automobiles with which buggies were beginning to compete. Buggy "auto seats" and "auto tops" looked similar to the seats and tops used on the early automobiles.

Fifteen quality features (or "points of merit") were cited frequently in ads and literature for John Deere Reliance Buggies:

1. Twin reach gear, double braced.
2. Cemented axle beds, double clipped.
3. Extra-heavy reach braces.
4. Straight-grain hickory reaches with channel irons.
5. Special wheel flange and hub, extra large in center.
6. Straight-grain hickory spokes and rims.
7. Extra-heavy steel tires set with hydraulic pressure.
8. Shafts with special heel and bar brace irons, all forged steel.

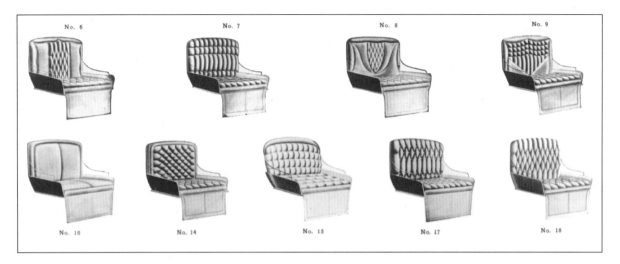

The customer had several buggy seat designs from which to choose. Shown here are 9 of the 18 styles available in 1912. The "auto seat" appealed to both young and old. The younger men appreciated the style; the older men liked the comfort.

9. Plugless bodies with yellow poplar panels, heavy sills, and posts.
10. Extra-heavy, over-lapping seat risers.
11. Special outside corner irons.
12. Seats and bodies extra wide and roomy with special seat irons.
13. Patented back stay and curtain fasteners.

14. Reinforced bow sockets.
15. Fine quality paints and varnishes.

Deere Discontinues Buggies

In his letter to stockholders in the 1923 Deere & Company Annual Report,

William Butterworth, president, made the following statement: "Owing to the falling off in the buggy business, the Company has discontinued the operation of the Reliance Buggy Company in St. Louis. Buggy sales in recent years have not been in sufficient volume to make the line a profitable one." Deere was now totally focused on the manufacture and marketing of farm tractors and a growing line of agricultural equipment, including wood and steel wagons.

Deere shipped buggies and other spring vehicles to sales branches and dealers in special railroad boxcars. This practice enabled the Company "to load and deliver goods free of dust and to the best advantage" — meaning undamaged.

Part II: Wagons

As early as 1881, Deere branches and their agents were selling wood wagons. In its 1886 catalog, the Deere Mansur & Company (Kansas City) advertised both "The Mitchell" wagon manufactured in Racine, Wisconsin, and the "Old Hickory" wagon from Louisville, Kentucky. Established in 1834, the Mitchell & Lewis Company claimed to be "the oldest wagon factory in America." Mansur & Tebbetts Implement Company (St. Louis) featured four different wagon brands in its 1893 catalog: "The Moline" from Moline, Illinois, "The Fish Brothers" from Clinton, Iowa, "The Wisconsin" from Racine, Wisconsin, and the one-horse "New Standard" from Cincinnati, Ohio.

Due to the demand for wood wagons during the Civil War, the westward trek of early settlers and gold seekers heading to California, there were hundreds of wagon manufacturers in the eastern half of the United States in the late 19th Century. Three manufacturers, however, were the main suppliers to John Deere sales branches: the Fort Smith (Arkansas) Wagon Company, the Moline (Illinois) Wagon Company, and the Davenport (Iowa) Wagon Company. By 1912, Deere owned all three companies.

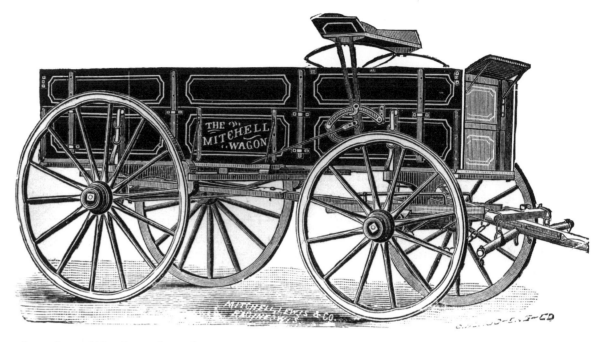

As early as 1881, Deere branches in St. Louis and Kansas City were selling "The Mitchell" wagon built in Racine, Wisconsin. With a steel spring seat and rear-gear brake, this wagon was priced between $100 and $125, depending on the wheel and skein sizes selected.

Fort Smith Wagon Company

The Fort Smith Wagon Company was an outgrowth of the South Bend (Indiana) Wagon Company. Wagon production began in Fort Smith, Arkansas, in 1904 and sales to Deere branches started the following year. Deere bought the Fort Smith Wagon Company in 1907 with shares divided five equal ways among the John Deere Plow Companies of Kansas City, Omaha, St. Louis, and Dallas, and Deere & Company in Moline, Illinois. The wagons built in the Arkansas factory bore the "Fort Smith" brand name. In 1910, Deere & Company purchased the shares owned by the branches and became the sole owner of the Fort Smith Wagon Company. Wagon production was moved to Moline, Illinois, in 1925 and the factory in Fort Smith was offered for sale.

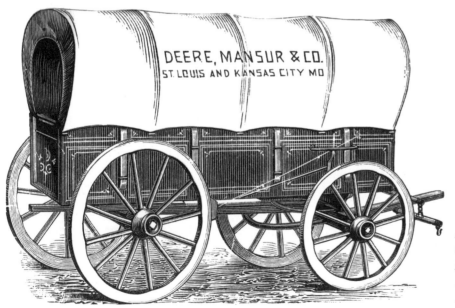

Deere Mansur & Company, Kansas City, included the *"Old Hickory"* wagon in its 1886 sales catalog. Built in Louisville, Kentucky, this wagon was priced at $105 *"with pole, bed, top box, whiffletrees, neck yoke and stay chains."* The seat ($5) and rear-gear brake ($12) were *"extras."*

As the logo on the side suggests, this farm wagon was built by the Fish Brothers Company, Clinton, Iowa. It was one of four different wagon brands featured in the 1895 Mansur & Tebbetts Implement Company, St. Louis, general catalog.

In the 1880s, many settlers were still *"going West"* and needed protective covers for their wood wagons. Deere Mansur & Company agents sold 11-, 12-, and 13-foot wagon covers *"machine sewed"* out of 7-, 8-, 10-, and 12-ounce duck material.

Deere & Company's Fort Smith Wagon Factory was located in the heart of the Arkansas hardwood timber country and surrounded by thousands of acres of oak, ash, and hickory trees. A Fort Smith Wagon was often called the "White Oak Wagon of Arkansas."

Moline Wagon Company

The Moline Wagon Company was started by James First, who had once worked as a blacksmith for John Deere. Originally, First was a wheelwright by trade. He began repairing wagons in the 1850s; then, with the help of a few hired hands, started building up to 10 wagons a week in 1854. In 1869, he joined Morris Rosenfield and Charles Benser in a partnership to form the Moline Wagon Company. A year later, First dropped out of the business.

In 1881, Rosenfield, who was by then president of the Moline Wagon Company, bought a one-third interest in Deere, Wells & Company — the Deere sales branch in Omaha. Soon Omaha and other Deere branches were selling "The Moline" wagon. More than one million "Moline" wagons were in use by 1909. With 500 workers, the factory claimed that it could build a new wood wagon every six minutes.

The Moline Wagon was sold by several John Deere branches before Deere & Company entered the wagon trade. The Moline Wagon Company was established in the 1854 by a blacksmith named James First who once worked for John Deere in his Moline Plow Works. In 1910, Deere & Company bought the Moline Wagon Company.

The John Deere Wagon Works was located in Moline, Illinois, near the Mississippi River. Prior to 1910, this factory was the Moline Wagon Company. In the 1940s, part of this factory became the Moline Tractor Works; and, in the 1950s, it was called the Industrial Equipment Works.

Deere & Company bought the Moline Wagon Company in 1910. Two years later, it was renamed the John Deere Wagon Company; then in 1913, it became the Wagon Works. From 1912 on, wagons built in Moline carried the John Deere brand name on both the rear axle and the wagon box.

During World War I, the John Deere Wagon Works prospered, due to orders from the federal government for military escort wagons, along with sales to farmers producing more food "to feed the

This ad for "The New Moline" wagon appeared in The Farm Implement News (a dealer trade publication) in the late 1890s. It was paid for by the Moline Wagon Company and listed four John Deere sales branches as "general agents." The purpose of the ad was to gain wider dealer representation and increase the sales of the Moline Wagon Company product line.

REPRODUCTION OF A BRIGHT-COLORED POSTER
SHOWING, IN A SCENE OF PROSPERITY, TAKEN FROM LIFE,
AS AN IMPORTANT FEATURE,

The New Moline
LIGHT RUNNING AND DURABLE.

SUCCESS AND THE NEW MOLINE WAGON GO HAND IN HAND.

Gives Satisfaction to the Dealer and Farmer.
Makes Money for Both.

GENERAL AGENTS:

John Deere Plow Co.,
KANSAS CITY, MO. and DENVER, COLO.

Deere, Wells & Co.,
COUNCIL BLUFFS, IOWA.

Mansur & Tebbetts Imp. Co.,
ST. LOUIS, MO. and DALLAS, TEXAS.

Deere & Webber Co.,
MINNEAPOLIS, MINN.

ESTABLISHED 1854   INCORPORATED 1872

[Registered Trade Mark]

THE NEW Moline

Farm, Mountain and One-Horse Wagons, and Teaming Gears.

MANUFACTURED BY MOLINE WAGON COMPANY
MOLINE, ILLINOIS, U. S. A.

As this trademark indicates, the Moline Wagon Company was established in 1854 and incorporated in 1872. The company was purchased by Deere & Company in 1910 and became the John Deere Wagon Works.

John Deere branches started selling the Davenport Roller Bearing Wagon in 1907. This factory was built in 1909 and purchased by Deere & Company in 1911. Steel wagon production was moved to Deere's Wagon Works in Moline in 1917 and this factory was sold to French & Hecht.

world." Between World Wars I and II, wagon sales rose and fell with the farm economy. The grain box with flared sides grew in popularity with the introduction of the mechanical corn picker. After World War II, farmers preferred steel wagons with rubber tires and auto steering. Due to a lack of sales, wood wagon production was discontinued at the John Deere Wagon Works in 1947; but the production of all-steel wagons continued to increase.

Davenport Wagon Company

While the Fort Smith and Moline wagon companies specialized in building wood wagons, the Davenport Wagon Company manufactured wagon gears and wheels made of steel. Wagon production was started in this factory in 1904 by Nathaniel French, G. Watson French, and J. L. Hecht. By 1907, all Deere sales branches were selling the Davenport Roller Bearing Wagon. The Davenport wagon had several advantages to offer the farmer customer: compared to

Here is an ad for the Davenport Roller Bearing Wagon that appeared in The Furrow *in 1909. As the sign shows, the wagon supported a 8,125-pound load, even though it had a rated capacity of 5,000 pounds. The copy claims that "the wagon never 'creaked' and the mules walked right along with the load."*

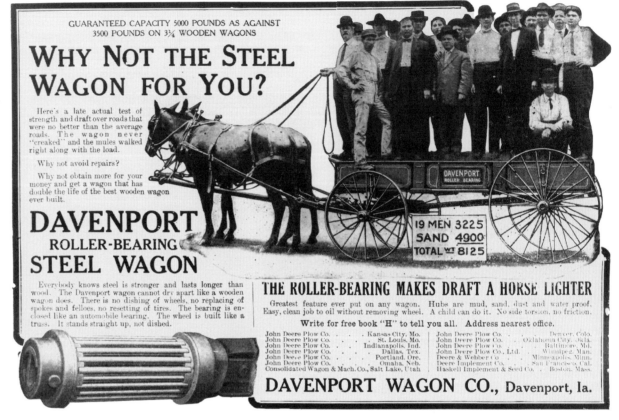

wood wagons, it had no "loose felloes" or "rattling spokes"; and the wheels didn't need to be soaked in water during long dry spells to keep the iron tires tight. It also was claimed in advertising that a steel wagon had a "one-horse-lighter" draft under the same weight load as a wood wagon, because the wheels turned more easily on roller bearings than on cast-iron or steel skeins.

"Built Like a Bridge"

Promotional material claimed that a farmer who bought a Davenport steel wagon would "never need to get a new wagon on account of having worn out his Davenport." The gear was made of steel I-beams, channel and angle irons; "the strongest shapes in steel structural work." "Like the modern steel railway bridge, they are built for the heaviest lifetime service."

In 1911, Deere & Company bought the Davenport Wagon Company and continued to operated it until 1917, when production was consolidated "for economic reasons" at the John Deere Wagon Works in Moline. Two years earlier, Deere granted the newly formed French & Hecht Company "the right to manufacture and sell steel wheels and wagon gear under patents for the Davenport Wagon Company."

Deere & Company dissolved the charter of the Davenport Wagon Company in 1917, which was a State of Illinois corporation. The French & Hecht Company

"Built Like a Bridge" was the way the John Deere dealers in 1909 described the Davenport Roller Bearing Wagon. The gears were constructed of steel I-beams, channel and angle irons — just the way iron bridges of that period were built.

The Name on the Wagon Has a Dollars and Cents Value to You

THE money you save on the purchase of your wagon, the profit it brings to you in the long run, depends not entirely upon the original cost of the wagon, but also upon just how important it is to the factory that the wagon give good service.

When you buy a John Deere Wagon, this is one big reason for your feeling certain it is a good purchase—the sale of an entire line of farm implements for seed bed-making, planting, cultivating, harvesting and storing crops of all kinds is affected by the sale of the wagon to you.

For over eighty years the name "John Deere" has been based on quality—the best that material and workmanship will produce. By selling you a wagon, or any other farm tool that is highly satisfactory, your friendship and patronage are more assured.

You will take pride in your purchase of a John Deere Wagon, not only because of its appearance, but also because

The John Deere Wagon Is Guaranteed

Right within easy sight, on the front end-gate of every John Deere Wagon, is a printed guarantee. This guarantee not only that the wood stock used is the best oak and hickory, but also that if—within one year from date of purchase—any part is found defective in either workmanship or material, it will be replaced.

Also, remember that John Deere Wagons are standard auto track— 56-inch tread—and they comply fully with the government specifications.

Inspect this wagon at your John Deere dealer's store the first opportunity you have. Write us for booklet describing it. Please mention *The Furrow.*

John Deere Plow Company
Moline, Illinois

(with which Deere had no connection) continued to manufacture steel wheels in Davenport for John Deere and other agricultural equipment companies. It also made wheels for John Deere two-cylinder tractors.

Wagons Advertised in *The Furrow*

Again, the different sales branch editions of *The Furrow* indicate which wagon brands were represented by the branches in the early 1900s, and also

show that most branches represented more than one wagon line. The St. Louis, Kansas City, Omaha, Dallas, and Moline sales branches advertised and sold three different wagons at the same time: "Fort Smith" wagons built in Arkansas, "The New Moline" wagon built in Illinois, and

The Moline edition of The Furrow *carried this half-page ad for a John Deere wagon in 1920. The guarantee that appears at the bottom was attached to the front of every John Deere wood wagon. A larger reproduction of this guarantee is shown on page 32.*

the "Davenport Roller Bearing" wagon made in Iowa. The Minneapolis branch also advertised the "Deere & Webber" wagon in *The Furrow*; and the John Deere sales branch in Winnipeg, Manitoba, promoted the "New Deal" wagon; manufacturers of both wagons are unknown, but thought to be the same. By 1920, nearly all Deere branches were advertising only John Deere wagons.

Three Wagon "Types"

The John Deere Wagon Company standardized the design and construction of wood wagons in order to reduce the number of parts needed and to increase the interchangeability of parts. Three basic "types" of wagons were built: farm wagons suitable for ordinary loads and rural road conditions; mountain wagons suitable for heavy loads in rough, mountainous country; and Western wagons suitable for intermediate service (between farm and mountain wagons). John Deere also built a deluxe line of wagons of each type known as the "Iron Clads."

The wood wagon front gear was made in two distinctively different configurations: either for a "drop tongue" or a "slip tongue." Deere even provided an attachment that converted a drop-tongue gear to a slip-tongue gear. As the name implies, the drop tongue could be raised or dropped to the ground; it was flexible

(continued on page 33)

This full-page ad for "The New Moline" wagon appeared in a 1909 issue of The Furrow; *this was one year before Deere & Company purchased the Moline Wagon Company. The ad copy points out that more than one million Moline Wagons were in use at that time, not only in the United States and Canada, but also in South America, Europe, Asia, Africa, and Australia.*

The "cut-under" design enabled this buggy to be turned in its own length without the front wheels rubbing against the body. Note the extra-high seat back which provided added support, comfort, and privacy for the passengers.

By 1912, the automobile had influenced buggy design, hence the "auto seat" and "auto top." A "quick-shifting top" meant that the top could be folded down or put up easily, even removed to make an open driving wagon — the forerunner of today's convertible.

This rural spring wagon was built for comfort, utility, and durability. Note the double elliptic springs in front and the four heavy platform springs in the rear. The body corners and top edges were reinforced with angle iron for added strength. There was sufficient room on the body floor behind the back seat for groceries, luggage, or a picnic basket.

Deere Vehicles—Styles of Body Decorations

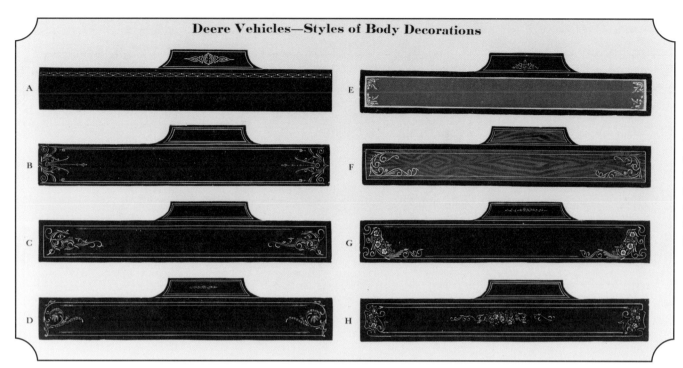

The bodies and seat risers on John Deere buggies and other spring vehicles were decorated to suit the buyers' desire for simplicity or ornateness. Several design patterns were offered.

John Deere buggy gears were painted one of four base colors: green, black, red, or yellow. Stripping of a different color was added in one of five different patterns: Sunset, Rival, National, Palmetto, or Southern.

Deere Vehicles—Striping Schedule

Numbers below indicate style of striping only.　Gear color must always be specified.　See Grade Description pages 8 and 9 for colors.

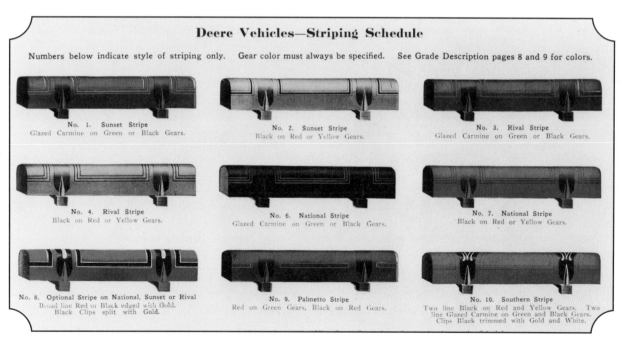

No. 1.　Sunset Stripe
Glazed Carmine on Green or Black Gears.

No. 2.　Sunset Stripe
Black on Red or Yellow Gears.

No. 3.　Rival Stripe
Glazed Carmine on Green or Black Gears.

No. 4.　Rival Stripe
Black on Red or Yellow Gears.

No. 6.　National Stripe
Glazed Carmine on Green or Black Gears.

No. 7.　National Stripe
Black on Red or Yellow Gears.

No. 8.　Optional Stripe on National, Sunset or Rival
Broad line Red or Black edged with Gold.
Black Clips split with Gold.

No. 9.　Palmetto Stripe
Red on Green Gears, Black on Red Gears.

No. 10.　Southern Stripe
Two line Black on Red and Yellow Gears. Two
line Glazed Carmine on Green and Black Gears.
Clips Black trimmed with Gold and White.

This John Deere delivery wagon was designed to haul up to 1,300 pounds. The side panels and top were well braced. It could be equipped with a 16-inch drop endgate, as shown, or with two rear doors. Note the protective side curtains, the heavy axles, and elliptic springs.

The John Deere "Iron-Clad" was a top-of-the-line wagon. It is shown here with three boxes. These boxes were 10 feet 6 inches long and 38 inches wide. In this illustration, the round "greyhound" trademark, formerly used by the Moline Wagon Company, can be seen.

This illustration of a "Fort Smith" wagon is from a 1912 St. Louis sales branch catalog. Deere branches started selling wagons built by the Fort Smith Wagon Company in 1905; Deere purchased the company in 1907 and continued to build wagons in Fort Smith, Arkansas, until 1925, when all wagon production was moved to Moline. Note the brake on the rear wagon gear.

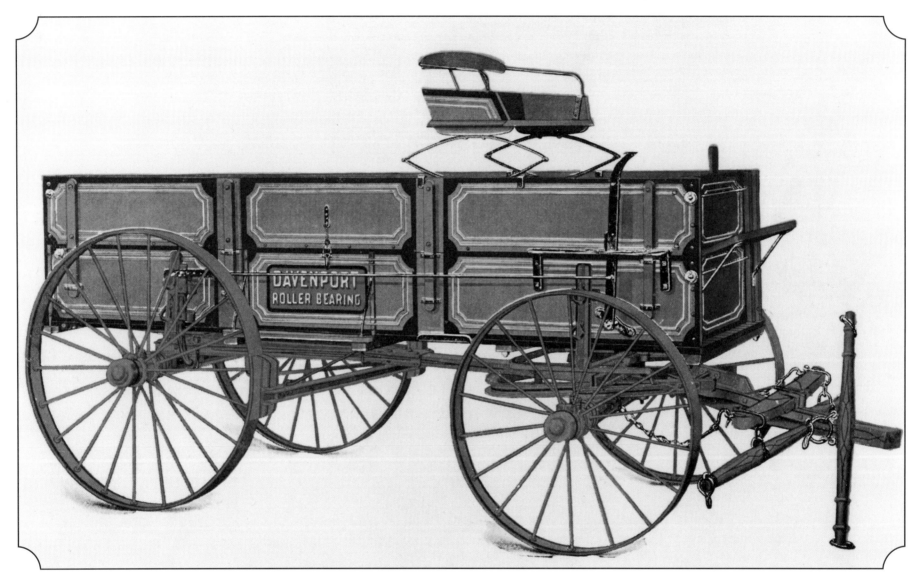

By 1907, all Deere branches were selling the Davenport Roller Bearing Wagon. This wagon with an all-steel gear was claimed to have a "one-horse-lighter" draft than an all-wood wagon of equal size carrying the same load. Because the gear was made of I-beams, channel and angle irons, it was advertised as being "Built Like a Bridge."

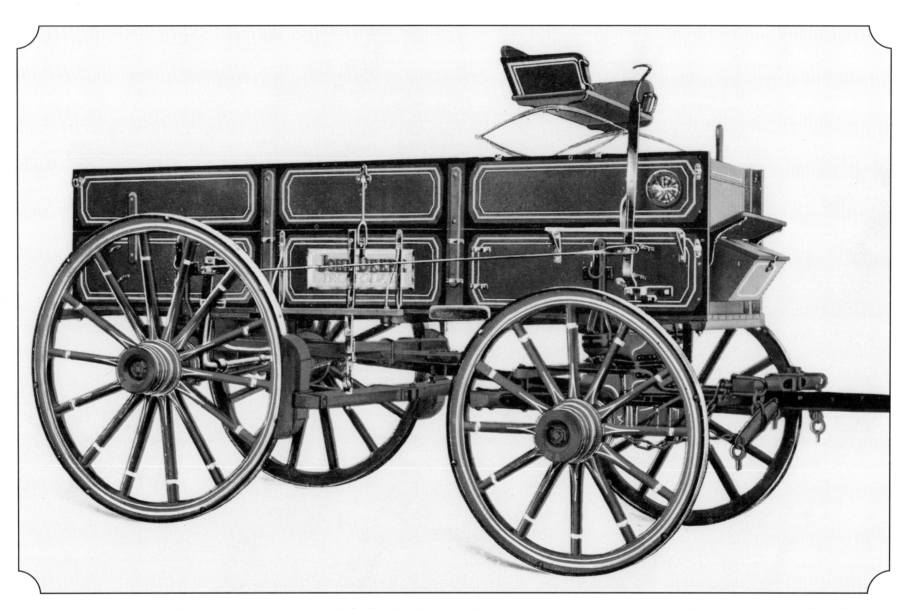

The John Deere Ironclad Mountain Wagon was built for hauling heavy loads over mountainous terrain. It was the type of wagon early settlers needed on the Oregon Trail. Note the tool box under the foot board and the iron rub plate on the bottom edge of the wagon box.

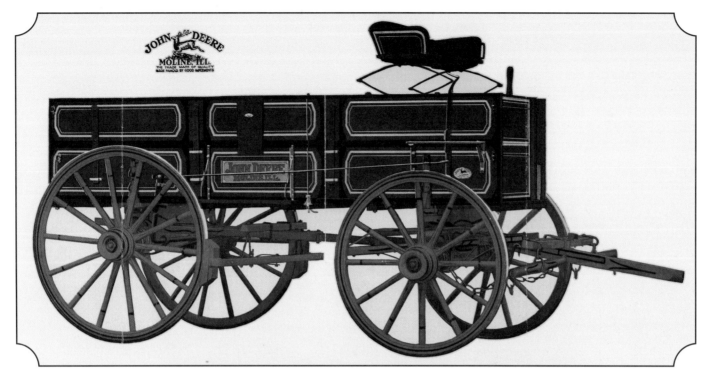

This "standard" class farm wagon was built at the John Deere Wagon Works. It was available with either a narrow or wide wheel track (tread) and had a rated capacity of 4,500 pounds. With 500 employees, the Wagon Works could produce a new wagon like this one every six minutes.

This colorful guarantee was attached to the front of each wood wagon. In addition to quality of material used and workmanship, a "light draft" was guaranteed, due to the wheels having the "correct dish," the axles having "accurate gather," and the skeins having the "proper pitch."

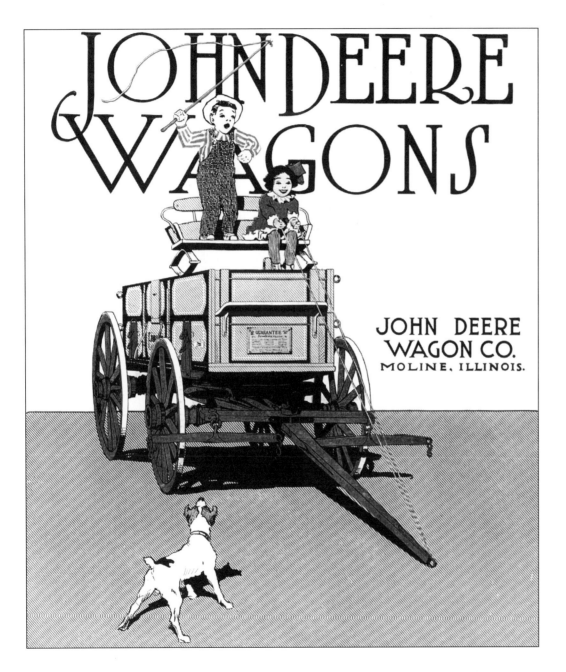

JOHN DEERE
WAGON CO.
MOLINE, ILLINOIS.

(Continued from page 24)
up and down. Farmers who frequently used two or more teams of horses to pull a wagon preferred the slip-tongue gear, because the tongue was held rigid (didn't drop); and the front team of horses didn't have to support the weight of the tongue.

Four Wagon "Classes"

Deere subdivided the three wagon "types" into four "classes": light, medium, standard, and heavy. The light two-horse farm wagon had a 2-½-inch axle for loads up to 1,500 pounds; the medium two-horse farm wagon had a 3-inch axle for loads up to 3,000 pounds; the standard two-horse farm wagon had a 3-¼-inch axle for loads up to 4,500 pounds; and the heavy two-horse farm wagon had a 3-½-inch axle for loads up to 6,000 pounds. Axles were made from air-seasoned, straight-grain, hickory stock.

The mountain and western wagons were designed for two or four horses,

Here is the front cover of a 56-page John Deere Wagon Company sales folder. It was not dated, but may be the first folder produced after Deere & Company purchased the Moline Wagon Company in 1910. It includes a description of each John Deere wagon "type" and "class."

depending on road conditions, weight of load, and steepness of the grade to be pulled: light mountain wagons were equipped with a 3-inch axle for loads up to 2,500 pounds; medium mountain wagons with a 3-¼-inch axle for loads up to 4,500 pounds; standard mountain wagons with a 3-½-inch axle for loads up to 5,500 pounds; and heavy mountain wagons with a 3-¾-inch axle for 7,000-pound loads. Oxen were frequently used instead of horses, especially in the West for pulling heavy loads up long, steep grades.

As indicated previously, the western wagon was designed for work loads between the farm and mountain wagons: medium western wagons had a 3-inch axle for loads up to 3,500 pounds; standard western wagons with 3-¼-inch axle for loads up to 5,000 pounds; and heavy western wagons with 3-½-inch axle for loads up to 6,500 pounds. There was no light western wagon.

Capacity Stenciled on Axle

In order for both the dealer and the customer to be protected and "not deluded" as to the strength and carrying capacity of any wagon purchased, every John Deere wood wagon gear had its "class" stenciled on the rear axle. For example: "LIGHT, capacity 1,500 lbs," or "HEAVY, capacity 6,000 lbs."

The neck yoke, doubletree, and singletrees were made of clear, straight-grain hickory. The eyebolts which held the wagon tongue ring were secured to the neck yoke by heavy iron bolts with a coarse thread. The singletrees were "thoroughly ironed" (reinforced). The doubletree had a malleable iron center plate and heavy steel clevises at each end. The tongue, hounds, and reach were made of air-seasoned, straight-grain oak. The hounds on the rear gear were extra long "to insure better following of the rear gear." The rear hounds also were steel braced for added durability.

Wheels Most Critical

Wheels are a wood wagon's "Achilles' heel." When the wheels gave out, the wagon was worthless. John Deere took pride in the way it made wagon wheels. Straight-grain hickory was used in the spokes and clear white oak was used for the rims or felloes. Spokes and "point bands" were hydraulically pressed on the hub. The iron band around the hub was electrically welded. Before the "hot" iron tire was set on the rim by hydraulic pressure, the wheel was immersed in

This illustration of an overhead wagon dump appeared in a 1911 catalog. The dump was used to empty grain into an elevator. This dump was built by the Marseilles Manufacturing Company, which was purchased by Deere & Company and later became the John Deere Spreader Works.

linseed oil to make it impervious to moisture. Wheel heights also were standardized with two options available for light and heavy wagons, and three options for medium and standard wagons:

	Wheel Heights	
	Front	Rear
Light and	40 in.	44 in.
heavy wagons	44 in.	50 in.
Medium and	40 in.	44 in.
standard wagons	44 in.	50 in.
	36 in.	40 in.

Wheels 40 inches or lower in height (diameter) were furnished with 12 spokes; 44-inch wheels or higher had 14 spokes. The size of the iron tire (width and thickness) varied with the "type" and "class" of wagon purchased, and with the width of wheel rim ordered. Five tire widths were available for a light farm wagon: 1-³⁄₈-, 2-, 2-¹⁄₂-, 3-, and 4-inch. These tires were normally ³⁄₈-inch thick. There were only three tire width choices for a heavy mountain wagon: 2-¹⁄₂-, 3-, and 4-inch; all ³⁄₄-inch thick. Initially, wagon gears were available with either a "narrow" 4-foot 6-inch wheel track (tread) or a "wide" 5-foot wheel track, measured from wheel cen-

ters. Later, an "automobile" 4-foot 8-inch wheel track was offered.

One-Horse Wagons

The John Deere Wagon Works manufactured both light and heavy one-horse wagons. They were available with either an auto track (56-inch tread) or a wide track (60-inch tread). Regular equipment included a "double" box 38 inches wide and 14 inches deep, a seat, and shafts. The light wagon was built for loads up to 800 pounds and had a box 7 feet 6 inches long. The heavy wagon with a 9-foot box was designed for loads up to 1,350 pounds. Both wagons were available with either steel or hickory axles; and both had 40-inch front and 44-inch rear wood wheels with steel tires 1-¹⁄₄ to

The John Deere Wagon Company built several different one-horse, wood farm wagons. This is a light, narrow-track model with a double box and spring seat. The box shown was 7 feet 6 inches long, 38 inches wide, and 14 inches deep. Additional boxes were available.

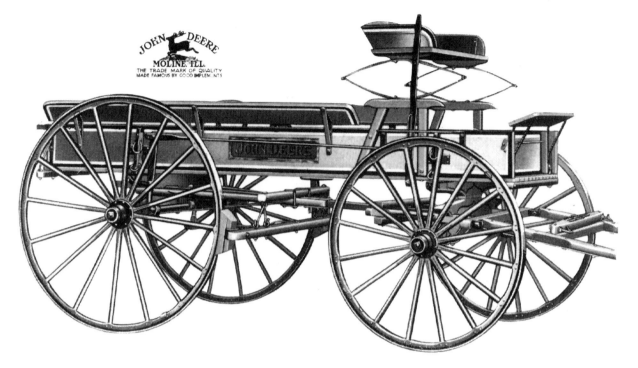

The John Deere Wagon Company built a line of one-horse wagons. The model shown here has a box 9 feet long, 38 inches wide, and 9 inches deep. The box also has flared side boards, a spring seat on risers, and a drop endgate. The wagon has a rear-gear brake.

3 inches wide. A "Business Bed" with short, flared sides and drop endgate was available for either wagon. A one-horse wagon was considered more rugged or durable than a spring wagon, but was not as "easy riding" or as "stylish."

Farm Trucks and Teaming Gear

John Deere had a line of wood "Teaming Gear" and "Farm Trucks," which would be referred to today simply as wagon gear. The teaming gear was built for loads from 6,000 to 10,000 pounds. The "City" teaming gear was available with 44-inch front and 50-inch rear wheels or 40-inch front and 44-inch rear wheels. These wood wheels had steel tires 3-½ or 3-¾ inches wide. The "Cut-Under" teaming gear had 36-inch front and 50-inch rear wheels or 40-inch front and 50-inch rear wheels. The "Cut-Under" gear was designed so that the smaller-diameter front wheels could turn under the wagon bed, enabling the wagon to turn almost within its own length. This cut-under design was preferred by city deliver people, because "U-turns" were possible.

Wood farm trucks were available with 30-inch front and 36-inch rear wheels or 36-inch front and 44-inch rear wheels, either with 3- or 4-inch-wide steel tires. Steel wheels also were available for teaming gear and farm trucks. Steel front and rear wheel sets were 28 and 30, 28 and 32, 30 and 34, 30 and 36, or 36 and 44 inches in diameter. The smaller-diameter steel wheels lowered the wagon bed

There were several different farm trucks in the John Deere wood wagon line. The model shown here has a drop tongue, 36-inch front and 44-inch rear wheels. It was available with either 3- or 4-inch-wide iron tires $\frac{3}{8}$-inch thick.

This wood farm truck was equipped with French & Hecht steel wheels with grooved tires and $\frac{9}{16}$-inch spokes. The front wheels were 28 inches high and the rear wheels 34 inches high.

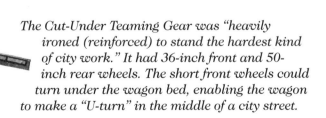

The Cut-Under Teaming Gear was "heavily ironed (reinforced) to stand the hardest kind of city work." It had 36-inch front and 50-inch rear wheels. The short front wheels could turn under the wagon bed, enabling the wagon to make a "U-turn" in the middle of a city street.

height and made loading or unloading easier. Early John Deere steel farm trucks had fifth-wheel steering; that is, the front axle, wagon tongue, and wheels turned together. With "auto steering," only the front wheels turn.

Special Wagon Gear

John Deere also built farm wagon trucks for special purposes. On the "light" end of the line was the Lettuce Truck which was sold mostly in California and Arizona. Designed to carry extra-bulky, light-weight loads, the Lettuce Truck had an 80-inch wheel track and a 12-foot reach. It had steel wheels 28 inches high in the front and 30 inches high in the rear, both with 3-¼-inch-wide tires. Axles, hounds and reach were made of oak, iron braced for strength.

On the extreme "heavy" end of the line was the John Deere Log Wagon. It looked like the kind of device a medieval knight might have used to storm a castle. It had eight, over-sized 36-inch wood wheels with 12 extra-heavy spokes. The wheels were 5 inches wide with ¾-inch-thick steel tires. The wagon oscillated between the four-wheel front gear and the four-wheel rear gear. This design enabled the Log Wagon to make a tighter turn than most four-wheel, two-horse wagons. The tongue and sills were made of 4- by 4-inch timbers and the bolsters (or bunks) were 9 feet apart. As the name implies, this giant John Deere wagon was designed to carry heavy logs over rough, hilly terrain.

The eight-wheel Log Wagon was the largest wagon in the John Deere line. Designed for hauling heavy logs, it had over-sized 36-inch wheels with 12 extra-heavy spokes. The wagon oscillated between the four-wheel front gear and the four-wheel rear gear, enabling it to make tight turns.

Skein Bearings

A "skein" is a wood wagon wheel bearing. Cast-iron and steel skeins varied in size, according to the "type" and "class" of wagon. A light farm wagon would typically have a skein size of 2-½ × 8 inches, while the skein on a heavy mountain wagon would be 3-¾ × 12 inches. All skeins were designed to be "sand and dust proof"; therefore, long wearing. A groove on the John Deere skein at the inner end of the hub was designed to trap sand and dust. A "wheel guide" or ring moved this gritty material to the underside of the skein where it could fall through an opening provided for that purpose. Nevertheless, wagon wheels needed to be pulled frequently so the skeins could be cleaned and greased.

The size of the wagon box, like the wheels, also depended on the "type" and "class" of wagon, or on the intended use of the wagon. A light two-horse farm wagon would normally have a box 10 feet long and 22 inches deep. The box on a heavy farm wagon would be 10 feet

This illustration shows the construction of a typical cast-iron skein cut in half. Even with the grease recess (B), the wheels on wood wagons needed to be pulled regularly, cleaned, and given a fresh coat of axle grease.

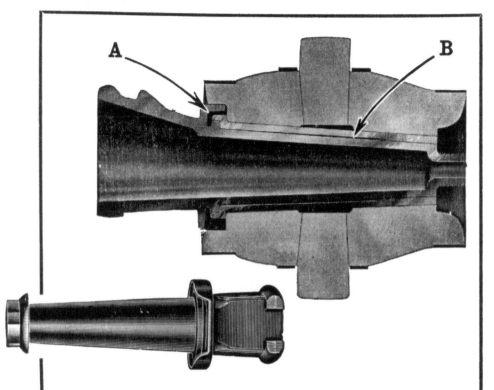

Sand- and Dust-Proof Cast Skeins

Skeins are of the special sand- and dust-proof pattern. They are fitted by special machines which automatically measure the inside of the skein and shape the axle to fit each skein individually. The skeins are set in red lead under heavy pressure, and each axle is tried for proper pitch and gather. In the illustration, above, "A" shows flange on wheel box, which extends over shoulder on skein. "B" shows the grease recess which insures perfect lubrication of parts.

(A)
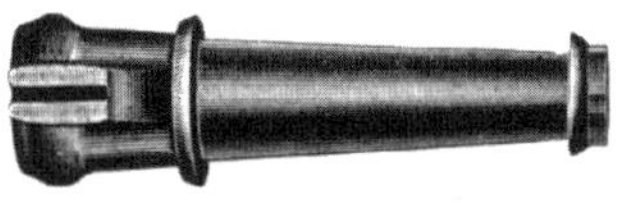

Bolted Truss—Moline Old-Style
Sizes: 3x9, 3¼x10.

(E)
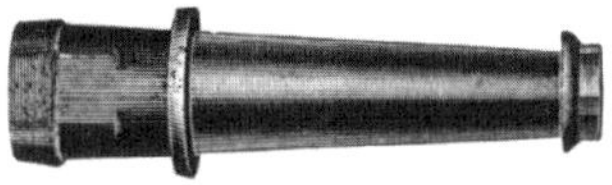

Small Bell—Moline Old-Style
Sizes: 2¼x6½*, 2⅜x7, 2¾x8½, 3x9, 3¼x10, 3½x11.
*Being used on present wagon of that size.

The skein was the wagon wheel bearing. It was made of cast iron or steel and came in a variety of diameters and lengths. The skein on a light farm wagon was 2-½ x 8 inches in size; while the skein on a heavy mountain wagon was 3-¾ x 12 inches in size.

(F)
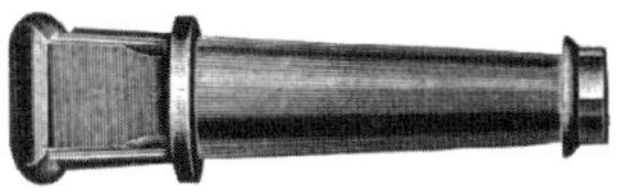

Moline
New Moline
Moline Ironclad
Sizes: 2⅜x7, 2½x8, 2¾x8½, 3x9, 3¼x10, 3½x11, 3¾x12, 4x12.

(G)
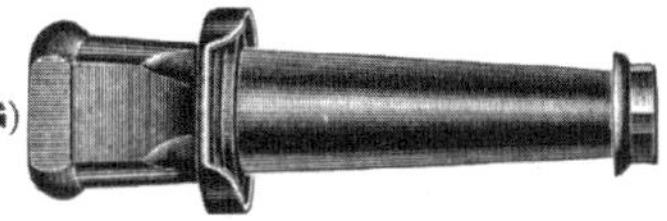

John Deere } **1912**
John Deere Moline } **to**
John Deere Ironclad } **1916**
Sizes: *2⅜x7, *2½x7, 2½x8, 2¾x8½, 2¾x8¾ 3x9, 3¼x10, 3½x11, *3¾x12.
John Deere Farm Gear—1914 and 1915
Sizes: 3¼x10, 3½x11.
*Being used on present wagon of that size.

(H)

John Deere } **1917**
John Deere Moline }
John Deere Ironclad } **1918**
Triumph Wagon—1917
Sizes: 2½x8, 2¾x8¾, 3½x11.

(J)
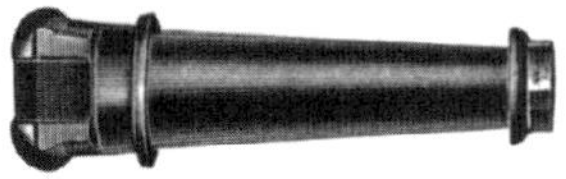

No. 36 Pattern
Moline Special Truck
Moline Universal Truck
John Deere Reliance Truck
John Deere Farm Gear (1912-1913)
Sizes: 3x9, 3¼x10.

(K)
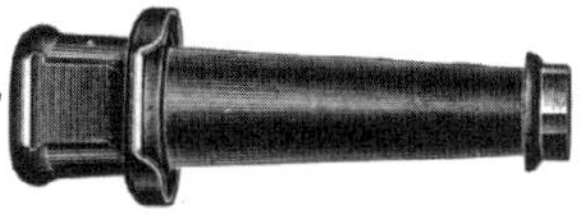

John Deere Farm Gear (1916-1917)
Triumph Wagon
Sizes: 3¼x10.
Triumph Truck
Sizes: 3¼x10.

(L)
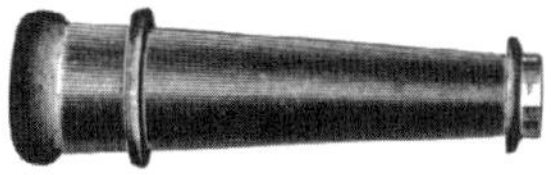

No. 35 Pattern
Moline Good Stock Truck
Moline Common-Sense Truck
No. 250 Truck } Sizes:
No. 400 Truck } 3¼x10.

6 inches long and 26 inches deep. The box on a mountain wagon would be 10 feet 6 inches long and 22, 24, or 26 inches deep, depending on carrying capacity desired and type of material to be hauled. Additional side boards (or boxes) could be added to the bottom box if needed for larger loads of lighter material. On a "narrow" track wagon, the box was 38 inches wide; 42 inches wide on a "wide" or "auto" track wagon. Boxes were also available 11 and 12 feet long. The longer wagon boxes required longer reaches. Deere boxes also were sold for use on other manufacturers' wagon gear.

Boxes were built of air-seasoned lumber. The bottom was made of narrow boards, tongued and grooved. The bottom was reinforced with five heavy oak cleats, more on a longer box. There was a double thickness of boards over the bolsters. Sides were strapped and braced; angle irons were used to strengthen the corners and tops of the side boards. Extra wide center panels on both sides were connected by a chain to prevent the sides from spreading. Two rods were placed across the top and bottom of both ends of the box to assure that it held its shape and square corners. There were one or two up-and-down iron tie rods on each side with a "malleable claw" at the top and a "tail nut" at the

bottom to assure that the sides were securely attached to the bottom. The standard bolster stakes were 13 inches high and the standard reach 10-foot long.

Options and Special Equipment

There was a variety of optional and special equipment available for wood wagons: 12- or 14-foot reaches were one choice, 11-inch bolster stakes another. There were various types of brakes, a seat, seat riser, foot board, tool box, feed box, boot end, shoveling boards, even steel wheels were offered as an option. There also was a number of different boxes and beds available, such as a grain box, narrow box, wide flat bed for loose hay, business bed for in-town use or a shallow bed with flared sides. The Reliance Buggy Company made special wagon boxes for the "Southern trade." These were narrow, 12-foot-long boxes for hauling hand-picked cotton to the gin or baled cotton to a river boat landing, railroad station, or warehouse.

Wagon brakes varied with the type and class of wagon, and with the load they were designed to hold. Most brakes were attached to the hounds on the rear gear. For holding lighter loads, a brake attached to the box bottom was available and less costly.

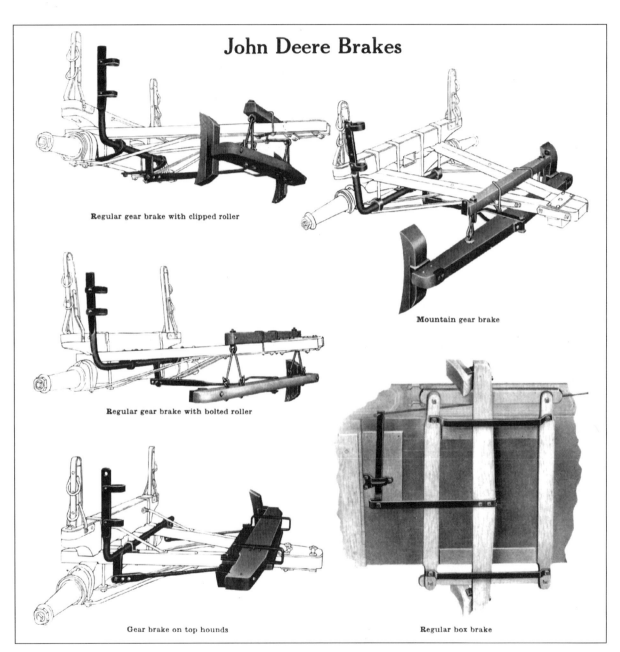

John Deere Brakes

Regular gear brake with clipped roller

Mountain gear brake

Regular gear brake with bolted roller

Gear brake on top hounds

Regular box brake

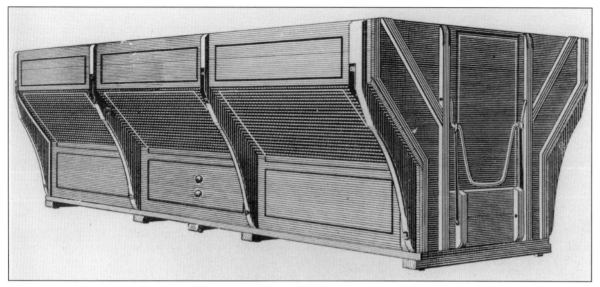

As early as 1911, the "flare-type" wagon box was used for hauling small grain. The box shown here was called a "North Dakota Grain Tank" and was claimed to be "flax tight." Note the endgate with a special handle for metering the grain flow.

Duplex bolster springs were available for wood wagons. The spring leaves were 1-½, 1-¾, 2, and 2-½ inches wide and 38 or 42 inches long. Springs were matched to the load to be carried. A set of springs with three leaves 1-½ inches wide and 38 inches long was suitable for a 1,000-pounds load. A set of springs with eight leaves 2-½ inches wide and 42 inches long were needed for an 8,000-pound load.

Triumph Farm Wagon

John Deere added the "Triumph" farm wagon to its line in 1914. Farmers buying this new wagon had several choices to make: It was available as a light, medium, standard or heavy class wagon; and as an auto track (56 inches) or wide track (60 inches) wagon in each class. The wide-track wagon also was available with either a wide (42-inch) or narrow (38-inch) bed. In addition, there were three wheel options: 36-inch front with 40-inch rear; 40-inch front with 44-inch rear; or 44-inch front with 48-inch rear.

The Triumph was constructed much the same as the heavier-duty or mountain-type wagons. The gears were clipped (attached) and braced at all stress points to avoid breakage or misalignment. The front gear had a large, steel, full-circle fifth wheel, making it a solid unit to prevent tipping or excessive rocking. The rear gear had long hounds to assure "true tracking." Both front and rear bolsters and stakes were "well ironed" (reinforced). The skeins were sand- and dust-proof. Each skein was individually fitted to the axle. The Triumph wheels had oak hubs, oak or hickory spokes, and oak felloes. Exactly the right amount of dish was given to each wheel to assure a light-running (low draft) wagon.

This new wagon was regularly furnished with a double box in a choice of seven sizes:

20 inches deep × 10 feet long
22 inches deep × 10 feet long
24 inches deep × 10 feet 6 inches long
24 inches deep × 12 feet long
24 inches deep × 10 feet long
26 inches deep × 10 feet 6 inches long
28 inches deep × 10 feet 6 inches long

All cleats on the box ends and sides were securely riveted. There were five hardwood cleats across the bottom and extra boards reinforcing the box bottom over the front and rear bolsters.

Introduced after World War I, the John Deere "Triumph" was advertised as "a wagon that will meet the popular requirements for a good wagon at a moderate price." It came regularly equipped with a 10-foot 6-inch double box, but the spring seat and foot boards were "extras."

This view of a Triumph wagon box shows that it had five hardwood cleats across the bottom and was reinforced over the front and rear bolsters. Note the up-and-down tie rod, the four side cleats, and the side panel to which the anti-spread chain was attached.

Bottom View

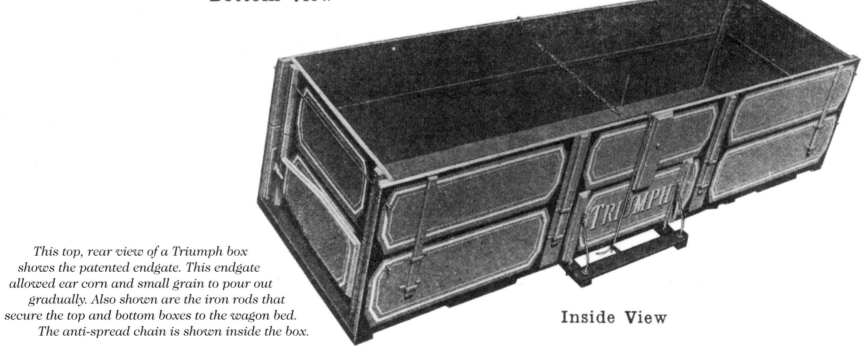

This top, rear view of a Triumph box shows the patented endgate. This endgate allowed ear corn and small grain to pour out gradually. Also shown are the iron rods that secure the top and bottom boxes to the wagon bed. The anti-spread chain is shown inside the box.

Inside View

Triumph Flare-Type Wagon Box equipped with patent rear end-gate.

The flare-type wagon box increased in popularity with the increased use of the mechanical corn picker. This view shows how the box sides were supported by channel irons and steel rods. Long steel rods on both ends and the anti-spread chain in the middle held the two sides together.

Depending on the box length, there were one or two pairs of up-and-down tie rods securing the boxes to the bed. Tie rods also extended across the front and rear ends of both boxes. The top box had a wide outside panel on both sides through which an adjustable chain was secured to prevent the sides from spreading under load. The Triumph box was carefully painted, neatly striped, and varnished to give it an attractive, durable finish. Depending on the box length and wheel sizes, a Triumph farm wagon with spring seat and foot board was priced between $128 and $146, rear gear brake not included.

This illustration appeared in a 1933 John Deere Triumph Wagon sales folder. It details the construction of a front and rear wagon gear, and shows a cutaway view of a John Deere sand- and dust-proof, cast-iron skein (wheel bearing).

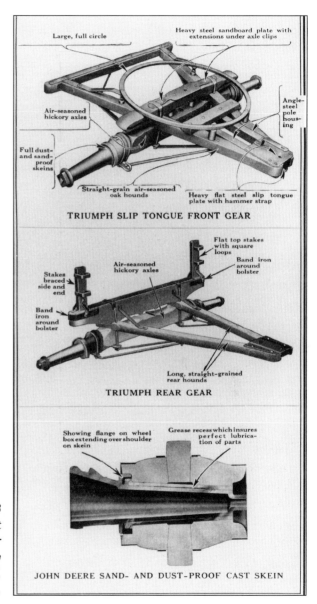

Large, full circle
Heavy steel sandboard plate with extensions under axle clips
Air-seasoned hickory axles
Angle-steel pole housing
Full dust-and sand-proof skeins
Straight-grain air-seasoned oak hounds
Heavy flat steel slip tongue plate with hammer strap

TRIUMPH SLIP TONGUE FRONT GEAR

Flat top stakes with square loops
Band iron around bolster
Air-seasoned hickory axles
Stakes braced side and end
Band iron around bolster
Long, straight-grained rear hounds

TRIUMPH REAR GEAR

Showing flange on wheel box extending over shoulder on skein
Grease recess which insures perfect lubrication of parts

JOHN DEERE SAND- AND DUST-PROOF CAST SKEIN

The Moline Lumber Company, which was owned by Deere & Company, built this saw mill near Malvern, Arkansas, in 1911.
The Rock Island Railroad laid 60 miles of track so logs cut near Camden, Arkansas, could be hauled to the mill.

Deere in Lumber Business

Deere needed millions of board feet of lumber to build wood wagons and other horse-drawn agricultural equipment. Through various subsidiaries, the Company owned or controlled thousands of acres of hardwood timberland in two states. The Fort Smith Wagon Company owned 7,920 acres in Sevier, Howard, and Little River Counties, Arkansas, containing an estimated 39 million board feet of lumber. The Moline Wagon Company owned 8,093 acres of timber in Franklin Parish, Louisiana, containing 46 million board feet of lumber. The Moline Timber Company, of which William Butterworth was president, owned 25,718 acres of timberland in Onachita County, Arkansas, containing 162 million board feet of hardwood. William Butterworth was married to a daughter of Charles Deere, he became a director of Deere & Company in 1893 and served as Deere's president from 1907 to 1928.

Logs from Deere's timberland were hauled on a 60-mile Rock Island Railroad track to the Moline Lumber Plant mills

The John Deere No. 802 All-Steel Wagon Gear was manufactured at the Wagon Works during the early 1930s. This gear had a rated hauling capacity of 4,000 pounds; this load of coal looks much heavier and undoubtedly had to be hand unloaded due to the huge size of the pieces.

near Malvern, Arkansas, to be sawed, cut to size, and stored for drying. As needed, the boards were planed to the dimensions required, not only for wagon production, but also for use by the different John Deere agricultural implement factories.

The 1923 Deere & Company Annual Report stated that "The Company has sold one of its tracts of timber covering about 8,000 acres in Sevier, Howard, and Little River Counties in Arkansas. This tract was remote from the Company's mills at Malvern and Smithton, Arkansas, and would require a considerable capital outlay before it could have been logged. The Company still has about 28,000 acres of timber and partly cut-over lands near its mills." The annual report also could have noted that iron and steel was rapidly replacing wood in the manufacture of agricultural products. Deere's lumber business would soon face the same fate as it's buggy trade.

Deere Steel Wagons

During the 1920s and 1930s, Johnny Poppers and other farm tractors replaced the horse. The popularity of the steel wagon grew with that of the farm tractor. The original Davenport Roller Bearing Wagon had fifth-wheel steering; it was later changed to "auto steering." In 1931, Deere introduced the No. 802 All-Steel Wagon Gear with "auto steering" and with several other new innovations. The auto-steering feature was a big change from conventional wagon design. It allowed for an exceptionally short, easy turn. It also was less tiring for the horses, because it reduced the jerking of the wagon tongue over hard, dry, rutted roads and fields.

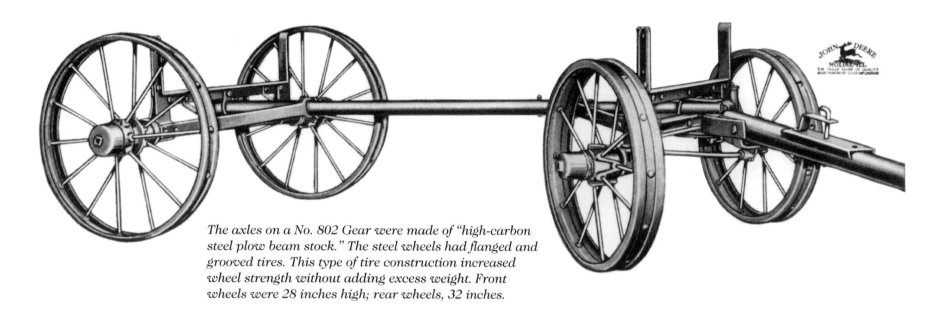

The axles on a No. 802 Gear were made of "high-carbon steel plow beam stock." The steel wheels had flanged and grooved tires. This type of tire construction increased wheel strength without adding excess weight. Front wheels were 28 inches high; rear wheels, 32 inches.

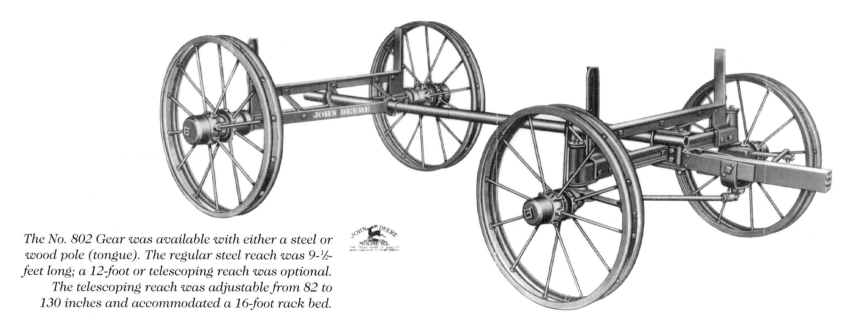

The No. 802 Gear was available with either a steel or wood pole (tongue). The regular steel reach was 9-½-feet long; a 12-foot or telescoping reach was optional. The telescoping reach was adjustable from 82 to 130 inches and accommodated a 16-foot rack bed.

DAVENPORT STEEL FARM WAGON

Rear Gear, with Brake—Showing Roller Bearings, End Collars, Linch Pins, and Axle Spindle, with Sleeve Removed

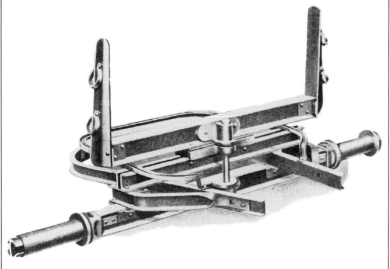

Front Gear, with Bolster—Showing Removable Steel Sleeves and Collars

Auto Steer   Removable Sleeve

No. 802 All-Steel Front Gear, showing Rigid Front Bolster and Stake Extensions.

Axle Bearing, No. 802 All-Steel Gear, showing the Removable Sleeve and Grease Chamber.

Auto steering and wheels with removable steel-sleeve bearings were important features of the No. 802 Gear. When worn, the bearing sleeves could be "easily replaced at small cost." Zerk fittings for a grease gun made it easy to grease these wheel bearings.

These two photographs show the construction of the front and rear gear of a Davenport Roller Bearing Wagon. The rear-gear brake was attached to the I-beam hounds. Note the size, shape, and bearing surface of the fifth wheel on the front gear. "Auto steering" was yet to come.

The steel wheels on this new wagon gear ran on removable "sleeve" bearings. When worn, the sleeves could be replaced at low cost "by any inexperienced workman, and without special tools." The front and rear gear were connected by a tubular steel reach. An 8-½-foot reach was standard; a 12-foot reach or a telescoping reach was optional. The telescoping reach was adjustable from 82 to 130 inches and could accommodate a 16-foot hayrack bed. The front and rear bolsters and stakes were one-piece and forged from high-carbon T-bar stock. The stakes were 9 ½ inches high; angle-iron extension stakes were available. This all-steel

When this photograph appeared in 1937, John Deere was calling its all-steel wagon a "Farm Truck Trailer." This wagon was available as a "regular" or "heavy-duty" model with or without bolster springs. It had roller wheel bearings, an adjustable, tubular reach, and auto steering.

The TRAILER that *Won't Whip*

ON THE highway . . . in your fields . . . whatever your hauling job, you can handle it faster, easier, cheaper, with this John Deere Roller-Bearing Farm Truck Trailer. It's a real general purpose outfit . . . safe . . . dependable . . . won't "whip" or "weave" like homemade trailers. It is strongly built and light-running—the outstanding achievement of many years in farm hauling equipment. You will want to learn all about this practical John Deere Gear. Built in two types: regular and heavy-duty, with or without springs; your choice of tire sizes.

ONE-PIECE BOLSTERS

HEAVY TELE-SCOPING REACH

FIRST-LINE TIRES

HEAVY-DUTY SPRINGS

AUTO-STEERING

TIMKEN ROLLER BEARINGS

DEMOUNTABLE WHEELS

REPLACEABLE BUSHINGS

TIMKEN BEARING EQUIPPED

JOHN DEERE ROLLER-BEARING TRAILER

wagon was rated for 2-ton loads. The front wheels were 28 inches and rear wheels 32 inches in height. Four-inch-wide wheels were standard; 5- and 6-inch-wide wheels were optional. The wheels had grooved tires. A wood pole or tongue was provided for a two-horse hitch. A wood or steel tractor pole with clevis was optional.

Rubber-Tired Wagons

In 1937, John Deere published a 112-page product catalog entitled *Power Farming with Greater Profit* as part of its 100th Anniversary promotion. A full page was devoted to the John Deere Roller-Bearing "Trailers" with rubber tires. No space was given to wood wagons; this was a sure sign that wood wagon sales were rapidly diminishing.

With the demise of wood wagons and increased production of steel wagons, Deere sought the best way to "position" steel wagons in its advertising. At first, they were called "Farm-Truck Trailers built for road speeds." Then "trailers that won't whip" was the slogan often used. Two years later (1939), steel wagons were "officially" listed in Deere price books as "Rubber-Tired Wagon-Trailers,"

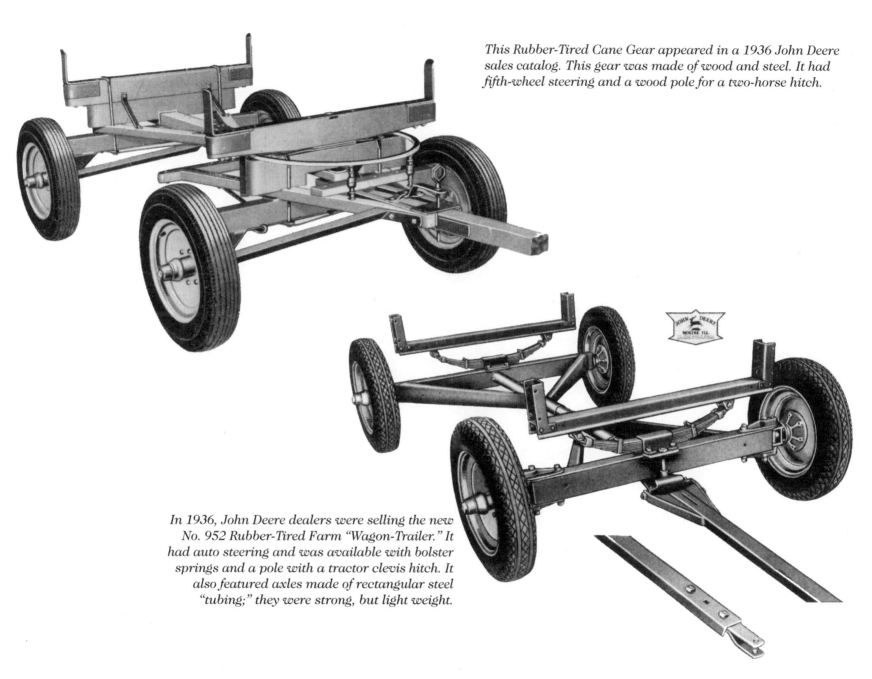

This Rubber-Tired Cane Gear appeared in a 1936 John Deere sales catalog. This gear was made of wood and steel. It had fifth-wheel steering and a wood pole for a two-horse hitch.

In 1936, John Deere dealers were selling the new No. 952 Rubber-Tired Farm "Wagon-Trailer." It had auto steering and was available with bolster springs and a pole with a tractor clevis hitch. It also featured axles made of rectangular steel "tubing;" they were strong, but light weight.

then as "Farm Wagons for Rubber Tires." After World War II, steel wagons simply became "Farm Wagons" or "wagon gear."

In 1937, there were two models of four-wheel, all-steel John Deere wagons. The No. 951 was designed for loads of 3,000 to 4,000 pounds. The No. 952 was a heavy-duty model designed for loads up to 8,000 pounds, "depending on type of tires and wheels used." Deere also had the rubber-tired, two-wheel No. 20 Trailer Cart for loads up to 2,000 pounds. Wheels on all three models were equipped with Timken tapered roller bearings, pneumatic tires, and demountable-rims. The four-wheel models featured heavy-duty springs, one-piece bolsters, a telescoping reach and auto-steering. These wagons had a steel hitch designed for use with a tractor, farm truck, or automobile. Deere promoted these wagons for "field work, fast trips to town, hauling milk or wood and hundreds of other jobs around the farm." In the mid 1950s, John Deere offered three steel wagon models: 943 Economy, 953 Standard, and 963 Heavy-Duty. Equipped with implement tires, the 963 was rated as a 5-ton wagon. In the 1960s, Deere added two wide-tread models for use with forage wagon boxes. The 1065

Wide-Tread Wagon was rated at 14,000 pounds and the 1074 Heavy-Duty Wide-Tread model could tote up to 10 tons. Extra equipment included rocking or

rigid bolsters, 10-leaf springs, and 4-wheel hydraulic brakes.

Other Uses for Wagon Factory

The John Deere Wagon Works in Moline, Illinois, was a very large, rambling, four-story factory. As sales and, consequently, the production of wood wagons

decreased, the factory had excess capacity the Company needed to utilize. In the mid 1930s, Deere decided there was a sizable demand for a low-cost, low-horse-power tractor for one-row farming or commercial gardening. Engineers at the Wagon Works were asked to design such a tractor. The Model "Y" in 1936 and the Model "62" in early 1937 were the first two pre-production "test" tractors assembled. In late 1937, the two-cylinder John Deere Model "L" was introduced. It was followed four years later by the Model "LA" and Model "LI," an industrial version. All three tractors were built in the Wagon Works. In fact, a portion of that factory was designated as the John Deere Moline Tractor Works, according to the 1943 Deere & Company Annual Report.

Wagon Works tractor engineers, along with engineers from the Waterloo Works who had designed the Model "H" tractor, formed the team that designed the Model "M" tractor. When the Model "M" went into production in a new John Deere factory in Dubuque, Iowa, tractor production ceased at the Wagon Works. That same year, 1947, John Deere stopped building wood wagons; however, steel wagon and harrow production continued at the Wagon Works.

Dealers today have a line of steel John Deere Wagon Gear to sell: the six-wheel 770, and the four-wheel 740, 720, and 700. Trucks have taken over many tasks once assigned to farm wagons, but there probably will always be a need for at least one wagon on every farm.

Final Assignment

In the early 1950s, Deere decided it needed a management group and factory devoted to the production of special equipment for its growing line of industrial tractors. The Wagon Works was selected. A new marketing and manufacturing team, including three design engineers from the John Deere Spreader Works in East Moline, was transferred to the Wagon Works. The Spreader Works engineers already had started to design bulldozers, loaders, and a backhoe for industrial tractors. When prototypes were approved, production was begun at the Wagon Works.

In 1958, the Wagon Works was renamed the John Deere Industrial Equipment Works. A year or two later, steel wagon production was moved to the John Deere Welland Works in Ontario, Canada; and there was no longer a Deere factory dedicated totally to wagon production. A decade later, the Industrial Equipment Works was moved to a new factory near Davenport and the old Wagon Works eventually was torn down. Today, a John Deere factory that manufactures planters and hydraulic cylinders stands on the sites next to the Mississippi River that both the John Deere Wagon Works and the Velie Carriage Company once occupied.

Here's a typical job for which the farm wagon is well suited. This wagon is hitched behind a John Deere 3950 forage harvester pulled by a John Deere 7600 tractor.

Deere & Company was in the buggy trade from 1899 to 1923 and manufactured wood wagons from 1907 to 1947. Initially, buggies and wood wagons were promising and profitable product lines, but times changed and both became obsolete. Dealers throughout North America still have a line of John Deere steel wagon gear to sell. Like the moldboard plow, the farm wagon no longer occupies the position of importance that it once held in the John Deere agricultural equipment line. In fact, in the current John Deere price book, farm wagons have been relegated to the "Miscellaneous Equipment" category, bringing to a close another chapter in Deere & Company's product history.

Appendices:

Sample Spring Vehicle Prices: Deere & Weber Company
Minneapolis, Minnesota (1900)

Description	Price
Buggy with top — 36-inch end spring, imitation leather trim, four-bow rubber top rubber-lined, green gear, black body decorated with green and red band, wire frame boot	$85.00
Buggy with top — 38-inch spring, 1,000-mile axle, felt pads, Bailey body loops, steel-cornered body, wire frame boot, trimming seal brown leather, brass buttons, padded seat ends, panel carpets, black body with mahogany panel, corner decoration, gear Brewster green, four-bow leather quarter top rubber-lined	$108.00
Concord Buggy with top — Leather trimming, 26- × 58-inch body, brake, leather quarter top rubber-lined	$150.00
Family Carriage with top — Three spring, cut under body, leather quarter top and leather back curtain, cloth trimming, lamps, and double fenders	$300.00
Spring Wagon with one seat — Light cross spring, imitation leather padded seat ends, 34- × 81-inch black body, red gear, riveted wheels, shafts	$86.00
Spring Wagon with three seats — Seal brown leather, black body decorated with green, green gear, riveted rims, 1-⅛-inch wheels, pole	$144.00
Delivery Wagon — Three spring, 36 inches wide × 7 feet long, 1-⅛-inch axle, drop end gate, yellow gear, black body, shafts	$86.00

Specifications for John Deere Farm Wagons (1914)

No. N. T.	No. W. T.	Capacity	Size Wagon	Size Tire	Box Length	Weight Depth	Gear	Comp.
423	424	1,500 lbs	Light	1 ⅜ × ½	9 ft 6 in.	18 in.	595 lbs	870 lbs
425	426	3,000 lbs	Medium S.	1 ½ × ⁹⁄₁₆	10 ft	20 in.	690 lbs	990 lbs
427	428	3,000 lbs	Medium N.	1 ½ × ⅝	10 ft	22 in.	710 lbs	1,015 lbs
429	430	4,500 lbs	Standard	1 ½ × ⅝	10 ft	24 in.	770 lbs	1,100 lbs

Steel axle construction in corresponding sizes furnished at extra charge.

Extras For Above:

Grain cleats.
Wide center panels.
Up-and-down tie rods.
O. S. top box fasteners on 9-ft 6-in. beds.
Deep panel seat with two-leaf springs.
Clipped roller gear brake.
Patent endgate.
Bow staples.

Feed box and bolts.
Bows and slats.
Ring and strap for four-horse hitch.
Gear brake with clipped roller.
Brake box connections (box hangers).
Gear brake top hounds.
Gear brake with reversible roller, lever, and chain.

Gear brake with reversible roller and short lever with rings.
Rear saw attachment.
Cumberland gear brake.
Lock chains.
Bent riveted rims on 2 in. and narrower tires.
Sawed felloes on 2 ½ in. and wider tires.
Bois d'arc felloes, regular lengths.
Bois d'arc felloes (short felloes).

John Deere Farm Wagons (1914)
Wheel Heights and Size Tires

| Size Wagon | Capacity | Catalog Numbers | | Tire | | Weight Complete |
		N.T.	W. T.	44 × 50, 40 × 44	36 × 40	with High Wheels
Light	1,500 lbs	423	424	1 ⅜ × ½*		870 lbs
				2 × ⅜		875 lbs
				2 ½ × ⅜		905 lbs
				3 × ⅜		945 lbs
				4 × ⅜		1,020 lbs
Medium S.	3,000 lbs	425	426	1 ½ × ⁹⁄₁₆*		990 lbs
				2 × ½		1,005 lbs
				2 ½ × ½		1,070 lbs
				3 × ⅜		1,040 lbs
				4 × ⅜†		1,175 lbs
Medium N.	3,000 lbs	427	428	1 ½ × ⅝*	1 ½ × ⅝	1,015 lbs
				2 × ⅝	2 × ⅝	1,090 lbs
				2 ½ × ⅝		1,115 lbs
				3 × ½	3 × ½	1,135 lbs
				4 × ⅜		1,185 lbs
				4 × ½		1,250 lbs
Standard	4,500 lbs	429	430	1 ½ × ⅝*	1 ½ × ⅝	1,100 lbs
				1 ¾ × ¾		1,165 lbs
				2 × ⅝	2 × ⅝	1,175 lbs
				2 ½ × ⅝		1,200 lbs
				3 × ½	3 × ½	1,220 lbs
				3 × ⅝		1,265 lbs
				4 × ½		1,335 lbs

* Standard size tire for each wagon marked.

† Wheels taken from another table.

N.B. – Medium S. approximates old style 2-¾-skein. Medium N. carries a heavier spoke, hub, etc., and approximates the old style 3-in. skein wagon.

Specifications for John Deere Iron Clad Wagons (1914)

No. N. T.	No. W. T.	Capacity	Size Wagon	Size Tire	Box Length	Depth	Gear	Weight Comp.
127	128	3,000 lbs	Medium N.	1 ½ × ⅝	10 ft 6 in.	26 in.	710 lbs	1,145 lbs
129	130	4,500 lbs	Standard	1 ½ × ⅝	10 ft 6 in.	26 in.	795 lbs	1,230 lbs
131	132	6,000 lbs	Heavy	1 ¾ × ¾	10 ft 6 in.	26 in.	890 lbs	1,330 lbs

Steel axle construction in corresponding sizes furnished at extra charge.

Extras For Above:

28-in. box, 10 ft 6 in.
Tool box.
Feed box.
Bow staples.
Bows and slats.
48-in. neckyoke.
12-ft reach.

14-ft reach.
3 × 4 reach.
9-in. tip-top box with grain liner.
11-in tip-top box with grain liner.
Drop pole 6-in. longer than regular.
Box brake.
Gear brake with clipped roller.

Brake box connections (box hangers).
Rear saw attachment.
Gear brake with reversible roller, lever, and chain.
Gear brake with reversible roller and short lever with rings.
Gear brake top hounds.

Cumberland gear brake.
Lock chains.
Bent riveted rims on 2 in. and narrower tires.
Sawed felloes on 2 ½ in. and wider tires.
Bois d'arc felloes, regular lengths.
Bois d'arc felloes (short felloes).

Wheel Heights and Size Tires

Size Wagon	Capacity	Catalog Numbers		Tire		Weight Complete with High Wheels
		N.T.	W. T.	44 × 50, 40 × 44	36 × 40	
Medium N.	3,000 lbs	127	128	1 ½ × ⅝*	1 ½ × ⅝*	1,145 lbs
				2 × ⅝	2 × ⅝	1,220 lbs
				2 ½ × ⅝		1,245 lbs
				3 × ½	3 × ½	1,265 lbs
				4 × ⅜		1,315 lbs
				4 × ½		1,380 lbs
Standard	4,500 lbs	129	130	1 ½ × ⅝*	1 ½ × ⅝*	1,230 lbs
				1 ¾ × ¾		1,295 lbs
				2 × ⅝	2 × ⅝	1,305 lbs
				2 ½ × ⅝	3 × ½	1,330 lbs
				3 × ½		1,350 lbs
				3 × ⅝		1,380 lbs
				4 × ½		1,465 lbs
Heavy	6,000 lbs	131	132	1 ¾ × ¾*		1,330 lbs
				2 ½ × ⅝		1,390 lbs
				3 × ⅝		1,460 lbs
				3 × ¾		1,505 lbs
				4 × ½		1,530 lbs
				4 × ⅝		1,580 lbs

* Standard size tire for each wagon.

Specifications for John Deere Western Wagons (1914)

No. N. T.	No. W. T.	Capacity	Size Wagon	Size Tire	Box Length	Depth	Weight Gear	Comp.
4127	4128	3,500 lbs	Medium	1 ½ × ⅝	10 ft 6 in.	22 in.	850 lbs	1,260 lbs
4129	4130	5,000 lbs	Standard	1 ¾ × ¾	10 ft 6 in.	24 in.	915 lbs	1,330 lbs
4131	4132	6,500 lbs	Heavy	1 ¾ × ¾	10 ft 6 in.	26 in.	995 lbs	1,420 lbs

Steel axle construction in corresponding sizes furnished at extra charge.

Extras For Above:

3 × 4 reach.
Mountain style bed with bow staples, tool
   box and long reinforcement over rear bolster.
If John Deere Moline, Ill., style bed is wanted in
   place of Ironclad, deduct difference in price of bed.

Grain cleats on Mountain style bed.
Bow staples on Ironclad style bed.
Tool box on Ironclad style bed.
48-in. neckyoke.

12-ft reach.
14-ft reach.
Deduct for California tire
   rivets not wanted.

Wheel Heights and Size Tires

Size Wagon	Capacity	Catalog Numbers N.T.	W. T.	Tire 44 × 50, 40 × 44	Weight Complete with High Wheels
Medium	3,500 lbs	4127	4128	1 ½ × ⅝*	1,260 lbs
				1 ¾ × ¾	1,325 lbs
				2 × ⅝	1,330 lbs
				3 × ½	1,380 lbs
				3 × ⅝	1,410 lbs
				4 × ½	1,490 lbs
Standard	5,000 lbs	4129	4130	1 ¾ × ¾*	1,330 lbs
				2 ½ × ⅝	1,390 lbs
				3 × ⅝	1,460 lbs
				4 × ½	1,530 lbs
Heavy	6,500 lbs	4131	4132	1 ¾ × ¾*	1,420 lbs
				2 ½ × ⅝	1,480 lbs
				3 × ⅝	1,550 lbs
				3 × ¾	1,590 lbs
				4 × ½	1,620 lbs
				4 × ⅝	1,670 lbs

* Standard size tire for each wagon.

Specifications for John Deere Mountain Wagons (1914)

No. N. T.	No. W. T.	Capacity	Size Wagon	Size Tire	Box Length	Box Depth	Weight Gear	Weight Comp.
227	228	2,500 lbs	Light	1 ½ × ⅝	10 ft 6 in.	22 in.	870 lbs	1,310 lbs
229	230	4,000 lbs	Medium	1 ¾ × ¾	10 ft 6 in.	24 in.	1,080 lbs	1,520 lbs
231	232	5,500 lbs	Standard	2 × ¾	10 ft 6 in.	26 in.	1,185 lbs	1,645 lbs
233	234	7,000 lbs	Heavy	2 ½ × ¾	10 ft 6 in.	26 in.	1,330 lbs	1,790 lbs

Extras For Above:

12-ft reach.	54-in. neckyoke.	Slip tongue.	11-in. tip-top box with grain cleats.
14-ft reach.	Patent endgates.	Bows and slats.	Feed box.
Extra length poles.	Angle steel grain liners.	9-in. tip-top box with grain cleats.	

Wheel Heights and Size Tires

Size Wagon	Capacity	Catalog Numbers N.T.	Catalog Numbers W.T.	Tire 44 × 50, 40 × 44	Weight Complete with High Wheels
Light	2,500 lbs	227	228	1 ½ × ⅝*	1,310 lbs
				1 ¾ × ¾	1,375 lbs
				2 × ⅝	1,385 lbs
				3 × ½	1,430 lbs
				3 × ⅝	1,500 lbs
				4 × ½	1,545 lbs
Medium	4,000 lbs	229	230	1 ¾ × ¾*	1,520 lbs
				2 ½ × ⅝	1,580 lbs
				3 × ⅝	1,650 lbs
				4 × ½	1,720 lbs
Standard	5,500 lbs	231	232	2 × ¾*	1,645 lbs
				2 ½ × ⅝	1,685 lbs
				3 × ⅝	1,755 lbs
				3 × ¾	1,825 lbs
				4 × ⅝	1,895 lbs
Heavy	7,000 lbs	233	234	2 ½ × ¾*	1,790 lbs
				3 × ¾	1,880 lbs
				4 × ¾	1,970 lbs

* Standard size tire for each wagon.

Specifications for John Deere Heavy One-Horse Wagons (1914)

No. Wide Track	No. Auto Track	Size Wagon	Capacity	Style	Length Box	Depth Box Lower	Top	Size Tire	Weight Running Gear	Weight Complete
522	521A	Heavy	1,350 lbs	Steel Axles	9 ft	8 in.	6 in.	1 ¼ × 5⁄16 in.	355 lbs	587 lbs
								1 ⅜ × ½ in.	415 lbs	647 lbs
								2 × ⅜ in.	426 lbs	658 lbs
								3 × ⅜ in.	486 lbs	718 lbs
520	519A	Heavy	1,350 lbs	Hickory Axles	9 ft	8 in.	6 in.	1 ⅜ × ½ in.	434 lbs	666 lbs
								2 × ⅜ in.	458 lbs	690 lbs
								3 × ⅜ in.	510 lbs	742 lbs

Extras For Above:
Steel-axle wagon with wood hub wheels.
Cross-bar pole with whiffle-trees and neckyoke.
Drop singletrees.
Gear brake with clipped roller.
Coach brake on bed.
Coach brake on gear.
Bow staples power set (16).
Steel skeins.

Specifications for John Deere Light One-Horse Wagons (1914)

No. Wide Track	No. Auto Track	Size Wagon	Capacity	Style	Length Box	Depth Box Lower	Top	Size Tire	Weight Running Gear	Weight Complete
514	513A	Light	800 lbs	Steel Axles	7 ft 6 in.	8 in.	6 in.	1 ⅛ × 5⁄16 in.	323 lbs	522 lbs
								1 ¾ × ⅜ in.	371 lbs	570 lbs
								3 × ⅜ in.	467 lbs	666 lbs
512	511A	Light	800 lbs	Hickory Axles	7 ft 6 in.	8 in.	6 in.	1 ⅛ × 5⁄16 in.	318 lbs	517 lbs
								1 ¾ × ⅜ in.	378 lbs	577 lbs
								3 × ⅜ in.	462 lbs	661 lbs

Extras For Above:
Cross-bar pole with whiffle-trees and neckyoke.
Drop singletrees.
Bow staple per set (16).
Gear brake with bolted roller.
Coach brake on bed.
Coach brake on gear.

John Deere Triumph Farm Wagons (1934)

Description	Price Factory	Freight
John Deere Triumph Farm Wagon – Standard Equipment		

56-in. Automobile Track with 38-in. Width Boxes

Wheels — Regular height 44-in. × 48-in.
Felloes — Narrow tire made only with sawed felloes. Wide tires with bent riveted rims, clipped and bolted at joints.
Box — Reinforced double bottom, front and rear, wide center panels on top box, anti-spread chains, angle iron grain cleats, patent rear end-gate. Foot boards. Four up-and-down tie rods. Six oak cross cleats.
Seat — Deep panel, two-leaf spring, no lazy back.
Equipment — Heavy malleable fifth wheel. Heavy sand proof skeins, square front wood hounds, full clipped gear, heavy flat truss roads, doubletrees and neckyoke.
WITHOUT BRAKE.

No.	Size	Tire	Wheels	Box	Price Factory	Freight
729A	(3 ¼ × 10)	1 ½ × ⅝	44 × 48	26-in. × 10-ft 6-in.	$127.50	....
729A	(3 ¼ × 10)	3 × ½	44 × 48	26-in. × 10-ft 6-in.	136.25	....

John Deere Triumph Gear Only — No Brake

No.	Size	Tire	Wheels		Price Factory	Freight
729A	(3 ¼ × 10)	1 ½ × ⅝	44 × 48	....	90.00	....
729A	(3 ¼ × 10)	3 × ½	44 × 48	....	98.75	....

Extras For Triumph Wagon

	Price Factory	Freight
Belted gear brake complete with box hangers	13.75	....
9-in. tip top box	9.50	....
11-in. tip top box	10.75	....
Add for tool box in place of foot boards	1.75	....

PRICES SUBJECT TO CHANGE WITHOUT NOTICE

John Deere Triumph Farm Wagons (1934)

Description	Price Factory	Freight
Northern Triumph Farm Wagon Standardized Equipment for South Dakota		

56-in. Automobile Track with 38-in. Width Boxes

Wheels — Regular height 44-in. × 48-in.
Felloes — Bent riveted rims.
Box — Reinforced double bottoms, front and rear, wide center panels on top box, anti-spread chains, angle iron grain cleats, patent rear end-gate. Four up-and-down tie rods. Six oak cross cleats. Foot boards.
Seat — Deep panel, two-leaf spring, no lazy back.
Equipment — Heavy malleable fifth wheel. Heavy sand proof skeins, square front wood hounds, full clipped gear, heavy flat truss rods, doubletrees and neckyoke.
WITHOUT BRAKE.

No.	Size	Tire	Wheels	Box	Price Factory	Freight
729A	(3 ¼ × 10)	1 ½ × ⅝	44 × 48	35-in. × 10-ft 6-in.	$140.00	....
729A	(3 ¼ × 10)	3 × ½	44 × 48	35-in. × 10-ft 6-in.	146.25	....

Northern Triumph Gear Only — No Brake

No.	Size	Tire	Wheels		Price Factory	Freight
729A	(3 ¼ × 10)	1 ½ × ⅜	44 × 48	....	92.50	....
729A	(3 ¼ × 10)	3 × ½	44 × 48	....	99.00	....

Extras For Triumph Wagon

	Price Factory	Freight
Bolted gear brake, complete with box hangers	13.75	....
Deduct if 9-in. tip top box is not wanted	9.50	....
Add for tool box in place of foot boards	1.75	....

PRICES SUBJECT TO CHANGE WITHOUT NOTICE

John Deere Wagon Boxes (1934)

Description	Weight	Price Factory	Freight
John Deere Wagon Boxes			
John Deere 26-in. box, with four up-and-down tie rods, and seven oak cross cleats, angle iron grain cleats, reinforced bottom, anti-spread chains, wide center panel with footboard	370	$33.75	....
John Deere, Moline, Ill., tip top box, 9 in. with angle grain cleats	....	9.50	....
John Deere, Moline, Ill., tip top box, 11 in. with angle iron grain cleats	....	10.75	....
10-in. tip top box with angle cleat	....	10.00	....
12-in. tip top box with angle cleat	....	11.00	....
John Deere spring seat, deep panel, two leaf spring, no lazy back	....	5.60	....
Reliance Wagon Boxes			
Reliance Wagon Box, 26-in. rear top end has an angle steel grain cleat, one cross chain four hardwood cleats on the outside extending from top of box to the lower edge of the box bottom, no tool box	325	28.25	....
Reliance tip top box 9 in.	....	7.70	....
Reliance tip top box 12 in.	....	8.25	....

PRICES SUBJECT TO CHANGE WITHOUT NOTICE

John Deere Wagon Boxes (1934)

Description	Weight	Price Factory	Freight
John Deere Draft Rigging Equipment			
No. 1961 crate containing six A-685 doubletrees complete with clevises and 18 A-20 singletrees, per crate	....	$26.80	....
No. 1962 crate containing six A-19 doubletrees complete with clevises and 18 A-20 singletrees, per crate	....	27.70	....
No. 1963 crate containing six A-19 doubletrees complete with clevises and 18 A-1395 single trees, per crate	....	29.50	....
No. 1964 crate containing six A-1416 doubletrees complete with clevises and 18 A-4246 singletrees, per crate	....	43.50	....
No. 2009 crate containing six A-685 doubletrees complete with 12 A-20 singletrees and six A-20 neck yokes	....	28.60	....
No. 2010 crate containing six A-19 doubletrees 12 A-20 singletrees and six A-21 neck yokes	....	29.50	....
No. 2011 crate containing six A-19, doubletrees, 12 A-1395 singletrees and six A-21 neck yokes	....	30.70	....
No. 2012 crate containing six A-4017, doubletrees, 12 A-4246 singletrees and six A-1399 neck yokes	....	46.00	....

PRICES SUBJECT TO CHANGE WITHOUT NOTICE

John Deere Beet Gears, John Deere Steel Gears, and John Deere Rubber Tired Trailer Gears (1934)

Description	Weight	Price Factory	Freight
John Deere Beet Gears			
No. 659, standard auto track, 40 × 44 wheels, 3 ¼ × 10 steel skein, 3- × ⅝-in. tires, capacity 8,000 pounds. No brake	1,020	$153.75	....
No. 661, heavy, auto track, 40 × 44 wheels, 3 ½ × 11 steel skein, 3- × ⅝-in. tires, capacity 10,000 pounds. No brake	1,095	165.00	....
Add for 4 × ⅝ tires over 3 × ⅝	110	10.60	....
John Deere Steel Farm Truck			
No. 802 steel trucks with 28- × 32-in. steel wheels having 4- × ¼-in. flanged tire, with horse pole. No DT or NY	591	59.00	....
John Deere Trailer Gears (902-S)			
With Telescoping Reach-Trailer Pole (#2989) Timken Bearings and with Wheels Indicated Below			
With JD-1046 (18 × 3.25 in.) wheels, with springs, less rubber tires	782	112.50	....
With JD-1047 (18 × 3.62 in.) wheels, with springs, less rubber tires	811	118.75	....
Note: JD-1046 wheels are for 5.25- × 18-in. and 5.50- × 18-in. R. tires. JD-1047 wheels are for 6.50- × 18-in. R. tires.			

PRICES SUBJECT TO CHANGE WITHOUT NOTICE

John Deere Beet Gears, John Deere Steel Gears, and John Deere Rubber Tired Trailer Gears (1934)

Description	Weight	Price Factory	Freight
No. 902 John Deere Trailer Gear			
With 9-ft Reach, trailer Pole, Without Springs			
With 5.25/18-in. rubber tired wheels	590	$147.50	....
With 5.50/18-in. rubber tired wheels	597	162.50	....
With 6.50/18-in. rubber tired wheels	630	178.75	....
For No. 902 trailer gear with springs, front and rear, add	100	19.00	....
For gears with regular horse pole in lieu of trailer pole, add	10	1.60	....
For gears with collapsible corn picker pole in lieu of trailer pole, add	11	6.25	....
For gears with 12-ft reach in lieu of regular, add	6	1.10	....
For gears with telescoping reach in lieu of regular, add	12	2.95	....

PRICES SUBJECT TO CHANGE WITHOUT NOTICE